EARLY CHURCH RECORDS

OF

BERGEN COUNTY,

NEW JERSEY

1740-1800

F. Edward Wright

HERITAGE BOOKS
2019

HERITAGE BOOKS

AN IMPRINT OF HERITAGE BOOKS, INC.

Books, CDs, and more—Worldwide

For our listing of thousands of titles see our website
at
www.HeritageBooks.com

Published 2019 by
HERITAGE BOOKS, INC.
Publishing Division
5810 Ruatan Street
Berwyn Heights, Md. 20740

International Standard Book Number
Paperbound: 978-1-58549-319-7

INTRODUCTION

This is a compilation of material published sometime ago and now out of print. We have limited our collection to records dated prior to 1801. One will wish to examine the original publications for records after that date. The first section deals with the records found in *Paramus Bergen County, New Jersey; Reformed Dutch Church baptisms 1740 - 1850...Records from the Gravestones in the Church yard, and a List of Church Members*. It was edited, index and published by Howard S. F. Randolph and Russell Bruce Rankin, Newark, NJ, 1935.

A collection of records of the Ramapo Lutheran Church was published in 1913 by the New Jersey Historical Society. These appeared in *The Proceedings of the New Jersey Historical Society*, Third Series, Vol. VIII, No. 1, pp. 1, and continuing in several succeeding articles. It was titled, "Ramapo Lutheran Church Records. 1750 - 1817. [Only the records prior to 1801 are published here. Ed.] It was noted that,

> "The Ramapo Lutheran Church was located at Mahwah, Bergen County, Jersey, about half a mile south of the present Reformed Dutch Church there. It was known as the "Island Church." The Lutherans were organized into a congregation some time between 1740 and 1755. They united with the Dutch settlers, and built the present Reformed Church. It has been somewhat modernized since then. The record here given came into the hands of Mr. Albert P. Smith, a very intelligent colored man who taught school for many years in the Saddle River Valley. He translated it and about twenty years ago handed his translation to the editor of these Proceedings, who revised Mr. Smith's version and gives it, slightly modified, herewith."

In 1948, Herbert S. Ackerman and Arthur J. Goff prepared a book called *Sesqui-Centennial Waldwick Methodist Church 1797 - 1947*. The church was earlier called New Prospect Methodist Episcopal Church. Those records prior to 1801 are included here. The authors noted that Methodist itinerant preachers visited New Prospect (now Waldwick) as early as 1791. "The first Methodist Church in Bergen County was organized March 1, 1797 and called Paramus Methodist Episcopal Church. The first church building was located to the rear of the Hermitage. ... The Paramus M.E. Church covered an extensive territory in those days known as Franklin township. It included parts of Rockland County, N.Y. It was then in the East Jersey District of the Philadelphia Conference which extended to this area until about 1826."

F. Edward Wright
Westminster, Maryland
1996

CONTENTS

PARAMUS REFORMED DUTCH CHURCH
BERGEN COUNTY, NEW JERSEY
BAPTISMS 1740-1800

Unless otherwise noted dates refer to baptisms.

1740

VAN ALEN, Gerrit and Eefje Neefje—Lea—Feb. 4.
Wit: Christiaan and Lea Zabriskie.

BEERMOOR, Lieven and Rachel Beermoor—Johannis—June 28.
Wit: Gerrit and Hillegont Van Blercom.

PIETERSEN, Salomon and Elisabeth—Susanna—June 28.
Wit: Salomon Dey and wife.

TYSE, Filip and Antje Worms—Pieter—June 29.
Wit: Diederik Wannemaker and wife.

BONGAERT, Lukas and Dorothie—Willempje—June 29.
Wit: Jan and Antje Bongaert.

VAN GELDER, Abraham and Rachel—Jacobus—Oct. 25.
Wit: Jacobus Van Gelder and wife.

RATAN, Paulus and Lybetje—David—Oct. 25.
Wit: Willem and Marytje Stevense.

RYERSE, Jacob and Marytje—Rebecka—Oct. 25.
Wit: Ryer and Betje Ryerse.

1741

WESTERVELT, Steven and Johannis (sic) Ackerman—Jannitje—Feb. 25.
Wit: Hillegont Westervelt; Jannitje Ackerman.

ODEL, Benjamin and Neeltje—Hendrik—Feb. 25.
Wit: Jacobus and Sara Stedg.

VERWEY, Laurens and Tryntje—Catryntje—Feb. 25.
Wit: Jan and Tryntje Verwey.

MEEKS, Joseph and Sara—Catryntje—Feb. 25.
Wit: Abraham Ratan; Sara Rutan.

DUGRAU, Arend and Angonietje—Molly—Feb. 25.
Wit: Jacobus Verwey; Molly Bon.

VANDEUSEN, Isack and Elisabeth—Jannitje—Feb. 26.
Wit: Willem and Jannitje Van Allen.

DEGREA, John and Hannah—Willem—Feb. 26.
Wit: Niclaas and Metje Volk.

WANNAMAKER, Coenraad and Diederik (sic)—Diederik—Feb. 26.
Wit: Marytje (probably the mother) and Anneke Wannemaker.

VOES, Hendrick and Grietje—Anna Marya—Nov. 2.
Wit: Niklaas and Marytje Muiseger.

ACKERMAN, Cobus and Dirkje—Marytje—Nov. 2.
Wit: Albert and Marytje Sabrisko.

MEAKS, Samuel and Yemyme—Joseph—Nov. 27.
Wit: Luwes and Mehetabel Konkele.

1742

VAN BLERKOM, Jan and Jannitje—Annatje—Feb. 13.
Wit: Jimmy and Annatje Johnson.

DUBOU, Andries and Jannitje—Pieter—June 26.
Wit: Pieter and Margrietje Dubou.

ACKERMAN, Johannis and Betje—Petrus—June 26.
Wit: Hendrik and Marytje Laroe.

BAARMOEL, Lieven and Rachel—Hendrikus—June 26.
Wit: Hendrik and Maretje Bertholf.

HOPPE, Hendrik and Catryntje—Rachel—June 26.
Wit: Pieter and Antje Ackerman.

GRUNIG, Abraham and Margryt—Obadia—Oct. 23.
Wit: Barend VanHorn and wife.

VOLCK, Nikolaas and Metje—Ariaantje—Oct. 23.
Wit: Hendrik and Ariaantje Volck.

STOR, Jacob and P. Wannemaker—Machiel—Oct. 23.
Wit: Klaartje Wannemaker; Maragriet Stor.

1743

ODEL, Benjamin and Nellie—Hannes—Feb. 6.
Wit: Hendrik and Tryntje Hoppe.

BOGERT, Cornelis and Lysabeth—Carstyna—Feb. 6.
Wit: Joost and Carstyntje Zabrisko.

BROUWER, Isack and Rachel—Marytje—Feb. 6.
Wit: Adolf and Maragriet Secoort.

ZABRISKO, Steven and Tryntje—Antje[1]—Feb. 6.
Wit: Abram and Jannitje Hoppe.

"A"

1749

ZABROWISKE, Jacob and Aaltje—Antje—Jan. 22.
Wit: Abram and Jannitje Hoppe.

VAN DIEN, Dirk and Catryntje—Andries, b. Jan. 9—Jan. 22.
Wit: Jan and Lisabeth Hoppe.

BANTA, Abram and Annatie—Abram—Aug. 31.
Wit: Teunis and Grietje Helm.

HOPPE, Gerrit and Hendrikje—Abigail, b. Sept. 14.
Wit: Jan and Aaltje Zabrowiske.

VAN HOUTE, Gerrit and Jannitje—Adriaan—Nov. 26.
Wit: Adriaan and Angonietje Van Houte.

TERHUYN, Dirk and Lea—Albert—Dec. 10.
Wit: Albert A. and Weyntje Terhuyn.

RIDDENAER, Hendrik and Grietje—Abel—Dec. 13.
Wit: Hermanus and Janneke Dugrau.

1750

WESTERVELT, Roelof and Tryntje—Abram, b. Feb. 7, 1750.
Wit: Cobus and Jannitje Van Voorhees.

VOLK, Abram and Rachel—Abram—May 24.
Wit: Abram and Caartie Rutan.

MEYER, Marten and Geertje—Abram—Nov. 18.
Wit: Abram Meyer; Rachel Labbagh.

DOREMUS, Hessel and Geesje—Annitie—Nov. 4.
Wit: Teunis and Annatie Hennion.

---

[1]It will be noted that from this point on the records were kept alphabetically in accordance with the name of the child.—EDITOR.

TERHUYN, Dirk and Lea—Abigail—Sept. 23. .
Wit: Jan and Aaltje Zabriske.
HOPPE, Jan and Lisabeth—Abram, b. Feb. 3, 1750—Sept. 23.
Wit: Abram and Jannitje Hoppe.

1751
VANDELINDE, D° Benjamin and Lisabeth—Ariaantje, b. June 18—June 23.
Wit: Hendrik and Ariaantje Vandelinde.

1752
VOLK, Nikolaas and Mettie—Arie—Apr. 5.
Wit: Paulus and Annatie Vanderbeek.
SPIER, Teunis and Cathalyntje—Annatje, b. Apr. 24.
Wit: Jan and Eva Amelman.
PILISFELT, Hannis and Marytje—Antje, b. June 14.
Wit: Andries and Antje Pilisfelt.
HOPPE, Hendrik and Wyntje—Aaltje—June 28.
Wit: Jan and Aaltje Zobriske.
ZOBRISKIE, Albert H. and Thellitie—Abram—Sept. 24.
Wit: Abram Ackerman; Marytje Zabriske.
BOGERT, Lucas and Dorotie—Antje—Dec. 17.
Wit: Cobus and Willempje Bogert.

1753
DEBOUW, Reyer and Abigail—Annatje—Jan. 1.
Wit: Cobus and Catryn Dubaen.
VAN BLERCUM, Lucas and Lisabeth—Annatje—Jan. 21.
Wit: David and Annatje Ackerman.
ZABRISKIE, Jacob I. and Aaltje—Albert—Apr. 19.
Wit: Marytje, wid. of Jacob Jan Zabriskie.
VAN SCHYVEN, Hannes and Vrouwtje—Annatje—July 1.
Wit: Wyntje and Hendrik Hoppe.

1754
VANDERBEEK, Abram and Saartje—Coenraad—Feb. 18.
Wit: Coenraad and Marytje Vanderbeek.
RUTAN, Johannes and Aaltje—Abraham—Feb. 18.
Wit: Abram and Saartje Rutan.
VAN BLERCOM, Gerit and Hillegont—Albert—Mar. 24.
Wit: Albert and Saartje Terhuyn.
DOREMUS, Cornelis and Rachel—Aaltje—Mar. 30.
Wit: Albert A. and Lisabeth Terhuyn.
CRIM, Fredrik and Barbara Krim—Adam—June 3.
Wit: Adam Aal; Antje Salomonse.
ACKERMAN, David and Saartje—Arie—July 5.
Wit: Hannes and Jacomyntje Ackerman.
STOR, Jacob and Grietje—Antje, b. July 10—July 28.
Wit: Andries and Antje Pulisfelt.
ACKERMAN, David D. and Annatje—Abraham—Jan. 26.
Wit: Albert A. and Lisabeth Terhuyn.

1755
TERHUYN, Albert A. and Lisabeth—Aaltje—Apr. 20.
Wit: Jacob J. and Aaltje Zabriskie.

HOPPE, Hendrik I. and Trientje—Andries, b. July 5—July 20.
Wit: Andries Hoppe; Aaltje Ackerman.

DENYK, Andries and Marytje—Andries—Aug. 17.
Wit: Hessel and Geesje Duremus.

TERHUYN, Abram and Marytje—Albert—Oct. 5.
Wit: Albertus and Anna Maria Terhuyn.

DUBAEN, Jacob and Marytje—Andries—Dec. 14.
Wit: Andries and Jannitje Debouw.

STORM, Staets S. and Belitje—Abraham—Dec. 4.
Wit: Abram and Aaltje Storm.

1756

TERHUYN, Dirk A. and Lea - Aaltje - Feb. 15.
Wit: Jacob J. and Aaltje Zabriskie.

DEBAEN, Jacob and Rachel - Abraham, b. Jan. 25 - Feb. 15.
Wit: Barend and Christina Kool.

KIP, Nicasie and Grietje - Antje - May 9.
Wit: Reinier and Antje Berdan.

WESTERVELT, Casparus and Martyntje—Angenietje, b. Aug. 14—Sept. 5.
Wit: Jan and Maria Westervelt.

HOPPE, David and Rachel—Andries—Sept. 30.
Wit: Hendrik and Wyntje Hoppe.

HOPPE, Gerrit and Elsje—Antje—Dec. 25.
Wit: Pieter and Antje Ackerman.

DEBAEN, Jacob and Marytje—Andries—Dec. 25.
Wit: Andries and Jannitje Debouw.

1757

DEMAREST, Benjamin and Wybrecht—Angenietje, b. Jan. 9—Jan. 26.
Wit: Samuel and Angenietje Sidman.

DEMAREST, Petrus and Maria—Annatje, b. Mar. 8—Mar. 20.
Wit: David and Maria Demarest.

TERHUYN, Dirk and Lea—Albert—Aug. 7.
Wit: Albert and Lisabeth Terhuyn.

ACKERMAN, Jan—Albert, b. Mar. 9—Mar. 19.
Wit: Gerrit and Rachel Vandien.

1758

GERRITSE, Hendrik and Neesje—Abraham—Sept. 10.
Wit: Jacob and Rachel Gerritse.

VANDERBEEK, Jurrien and Marietje—Arie—Nov. 12.
Wit: Hans A. and Jacomyn Ackerman.

HOPPE, Albert and Rachel—Abraham—Nov. 9.
Wit: Abram and Jacomyntje Alyie.

ACKERMAN, David D. and Annatje—Annatje—Nov. 19.
Wit: Gerrit D. and Lena Ackerman.

ZABRISKIE, Jacob H. and Wyntje—Antje—Feb. 5.
Wit: Dirk and Antje Terhuyn.

1759

HOPPE, Andries J. and Marytje—Antje—Apr. 9.
Wit: Nicklaas and Semme (?) Demarest.

STORM, Abram and Aaltje—Annatje, b. June 21—July 22.
Wit: David H. Ackerman; Annatje C. Demarest.

VANDERBEEK, Abram and Sara—Abram, b. June 26.
Wit: Abram A. and Lena Ackerman.
ACKERMAN, Gerrit D. and Lena—Abraham—Sept. 3.
Wit: Hannes H. and Lena Ackerman.
TERHUYN, Dirk and Lea—Andries—Sept. 23.
Wit: Andries H. and Antje Hoppe.
CADMUS, Fredrik and Saartje—Abram, b. Nov. 27—Dec. 25.
Wit: Abram and Lea (?) Cadmus.

1760
VANDIEN, Gerrit and Saartje—Albert—Feb. 17.
Wit: Jan Ackerman; Rachel Vandien.
SIDMAN, Samuel and Angonietje—Angonietje—Mar. 30.
Wit: Willem and Catrina Syourt.
POST, Frans A. and Rachel—Aaltje, b. Feb. 7.—Apr. 13.
Wit: Cornelis Y. and Janneke Westervelt.
ZABRISKIE, Jacob H. and Wyntje—Albert—Oct. 18.
Wit: Albert H. and Thellitie Zabriskie.
LUTKENS, Hendrik and Lybe—Antje—Dec. 4.
Wit: Jan and Belitje Deremus.

1761
BOGART, Cobus and Cornelia—Antje—Jan. 24.
Wit: Antje and Steven Bogert.
STORM, Hendrik and Cornelia—Angonietje—Mar. 29.
Wit: Jacob and Saartje Hoppe.
HOPPE, Marytje—Andries—Apr. 12.
Wit: Hendrik I. and Trientje Hoppe.
ZABRISKIE, Jacob I. and Jannitje—Aaltje—June 14.
Wit: Jan and Aaltje Zabriskie.
VERSEUR, Johannis and Lena—Abraham, b. June 26—Aug. 2.
Wit: Abram and Annatje Banta.
ACKERMAN, Hannes and Jacomyntje—Arie—Sept. 1.
Wit: Arie and Ariaantje Ackerman.
ACKERMAN, Gerrit D. and Lena—Abigael—Dec. 20.
Wit: Lambertus and Lybe Laroi.

1762
WRITE, Willem and Aaltje—Albert—Feb. 14.
Wit: Albert C. and Aaltje Zabriske.
POST, Hannes and Catrintje—Abram—Feb. 14.
Wit: Abram and Saartje Rutan.
TERHUYN, Dirk and Lea—Abraham—Mar. 20.
Wit: Abram and Marytje Terhuyn.
HOPPE, David and Rachel—Ariaantje, b. Apr. 6—Apr. 25.
Wit: Hannes and Ariaantje Van Emburgh.
VANDIEN, Gerrit and Sara—Antje—Oct. 17.
Wit: Hendrik and Lybe Lutkens.
ZABRISKE, Jacob H. and Wyntje—Aaltje—Oct. 31.
Wit: Jacob I. and Aaltje Zabriske.

1763
BOGERT, Steven and Rachel—Antje—Jan. 9.
Wit: Cobus and Cornelia Bogert.

WESTERVELT, Roelof and Tryntje—Albert—Apr. 17.
Wit: Albert and Rachel Ackerman.
PILESFELT, Willem and Lisabeth—Abram, b. Aug. 1—Aug. 21.
Wit: Abram A. and Lena Ackerman.

1764

HOPPE, Jacob and Saartje—Abram, b. Jan. 11—Feb. 19.
Wit: Abram and Rebecka Hoppe.
SYOURT, Willem and Catrina—Adolf, b. June 8—July 8.
Wit: Hannes and Lisabeth Syourt.
DUBAEN, Jacob and Marietje—Antje—Oct. 28.
Wit: David D. and Annatje Ackerman.
ECKERSEN, David and Angenietje—Annatje, b. Aug. 15—Sept. 2.

1765

TOIRS, Laurens and Lisabeth—Arie, b. Jan. 6—Jan. 10.
Wit: Jurrien and Marytje Vanderbeek.
WRITE, Willem and Aaltje—Abram— Apr. 28.
Wit: Gerrit and Sara Van Dien.
VAN ZEYL, Petrus and Jannitje—Abram—Apr. 28.
Wit: Hendrik and Marytje Messiker.
FERSEUR, Hannes and Lena—Annatje, b. May 4—May 26.
Wit: Abram and Annatje Banta.
HOPPE, Andries A. and Lisbeth—Abraham—June 23.
Wit: Abram and Rebecka Hoppe.
ACKERMAN, Abram and Marytje—Antje—Oct. 22.
Wit: Jan J. Zabriske; Wyntje Hoppe.
BANTA, Cornelis A. and Maria—Annatje—Nov. —.
Wit: Jacob and Annaatje Banta.
BOGERT, Jacob and Marytje—Annatje—Nov. 24.
Wit: Cobus and Willempje Rutan.
TERHUYN, Samuel and Lea—Antje—Dec. 19.
Wit: Albert and Sara Terhuyn.
KUYPER, Abram and Sara—Abram, b. Mar. 26—Apr. 27.
Wit: Daniel and Lisabeth Blauvelt.
ACKERMAN, David A. and Myntje—Abram, b. June 15—June 29.
Wit: Abram J. and Brechtje Ackerman.
BANTA, Jan and Lena—Antje, b. Oct. 21—Nov. 16.
Wit: Paulus and Jannitje Rutan.

1767

VAN ORDEN, Jan and Jannetje—Aaltje—Jan. 4.
Wit: Hendrik and Marietje Oldes.
ACKERMAN, David J. and Nietie—Antje—Jan. 18.
Wit: Cobus and Cornelia Bogert.
BANTA, Samuel and Lisabeth—Abram, b. Apr. 13—May 3.
Wit: Johannis and Lena Verscheur.
PIETERSE, Niklaas and Maria—Andries, b. Apr. 18—May 17.
Wit: Andries and Saartje Pieterse.
ACKERMAN, Willem and Grietje—Albert—Apr. 24.
Wit: Albert V. and Marytje Voorhees.
BROUWER, Abram D.—Abram—July 19.
Wit: Abram and Saartje Rutan.

WOERTENDYK, Rynier and wife—Aaltje—July 19.
Wit: Frederik and Jemyma Woertendyk.
HOPPE, Albert and Rachel—Andries—Sept. 27.
Wit: Johannes J. and Lena Ackerman.
BOGERT, Petrus P. and Maria—Abram—Nov. 15.
Wit: Abram J. and Brechje Ackerman.
VAN BLERCOM, Pieter H. and Jannitje—Aaltje—Nov. 15.
Wit: David H. and Antje P. Van blerkom.

1768
TERHUYN, Dirk A. and Lea—Andries—Mar. 6.
Wit: Andries J. and Cristina Zabriske.
HOPPE, Abram H. and Antje—Aaltje—Aug. 7.
Wit: Jacob J. and Aaltje Zabriske.
JACOBUSSE, Brand B. and Geertje—Antje—Sept. 19.
Wit: Pieter and Trientje Van Wagene.

1767
DEVOE, Jan and Aaltje—Abraham—May 3.

1768
STORM, Hendrik and Cornelia—Abram—Nov. 13.
Wit: Andries A. Hoppe and Marytje Hoppe.
CHRISTIE, Andries and Abigail—Antje, b. Nov. 26—Dec. 25.
Wit: Willem and Antje Hoppe.
WESSELS, Joseph and Ariaantje—Ariaantje—Dec. 25.
Wit: Hendrik and Marytje Oldes.
VESEUR, Barend and Syntje—Annatje—Dec. 25.
Wit: Gerrit and Annatje Blauvelt.

1769
WOERTENDYK, Rynier and his 2nd wife—Albert, b. Jan. 23—Feb. 5.
ECKERSEN, David and Angonietje—Angonietje, b. Jan. 11—Feb. 26.
Wit: Paulus C. and Annatje Vanderbeek.
ALYE, Albert and Maria—Albert—Mar. 12.
Wit: Albert and Rachel Hoppe.
BOGERT, Steven and Rachel—Antje, b. June 20—July 2.
Wit: Jan and Willempje Dumaree.
STAGG, Isaac and Helena—Abraham—Aug. 27.
Wit: Thomas and Geertje Banta.
HOPPE, Andries A. and Marytje—Andries—Sept. 3.
Wit: Andries I. and Elisabeth Hoppe.
RUTAN, Johannis P. and Cathalyntje—Abraham—Sept. 1.
Wit: Abraham and Saartje Rutan.
HENNION, David D. and Tryntje—Andries—Oct. 15.
Wit: Elisabeth and Johannis Hennion.
ZABRISKE, Jacob J. and Jannitje—Antje—Nov. 5.
Wit: Jan J. and Lea Zabriskie.
HOPPE, David and Rachel—Abigail, b. Nov. 26—Nov. 30.
Wit: Jan and Aaltje Zabriske.
RUTAN, Pieter and Jannetje—Abraham—Dec. 24.
Wit: Abram W. and Grietje Rutan.
HOPPE, Gerret H. and Antje—Albert—Dec. 24.
Wit: Andries A. and Jannetje Zabriskie.

1770

RYKER, Hendrik and Grace—Abraham—Jan. 14.
Wit: Abraham and Polly Bricker.

BANTA, Jacob and Rachel—Abram, Jan. 14.

HOPPE, Jan J. and Geertje—Andries—Mar. 25.
Wit: Abram and Marytje Ackerman.

DUMAREE, Albert C. and Rachel—Albert, b. June 19—July 8.
Wit: Albert and Lea Deryie.

DUBAEN, Abram and Brechje—Abraham, b. June 14—July 8.
Wit: Christiaen and Rachel Dubaen.

TERHUYN, Dirk and Lea—Albert—July 29.
Wit: Albert A. and Betje Terhuyn.

RUTAN, Cobus and Willempje—Albert—Aug. 24.
Wit: Albert and Machtel Bogert.

ZABRISKIE, Jan J. and Lea—Aaltje—Sept. 30.
Wit: Jan and Aaltje Zabriske.

LUTKENS, Pieter and Lisabeth—Antje—Sept. 30.
Wit: Harme H. and Antie Lutkens.

SUDDERLAND, James and Marietje—Antje—Dec. 6.
Wit: Jan and Lea Maybe.

WINTER, Hannes and Sara—Abram—Dec. 9.
Wit: Abram V. Voorheesen.

1771

PERRIE, Cobus and Annatje—Annatje—Feb. 24.
Wit: Daniel and Jannetje Perrie.

VAN BLERKOM, Isaac and Saartje—Annatje—Feb. 24.
Wit: Jonathan and Annatje Wealer.

QUACKENBOS, Abram and Gerritie—Anna Elisabeth, b. May 23—June 23.
Wit: Abram C. Herring; Wyntje Quackenbos.

DUMAREE, Samuel B. and Rebecka—Annatje—June 30.
Wit: David and Annatje Dumaree.

DUREMES, Johannes and Jannitje—Abraham, b. Oct. 3—Nov. 3.
Wit: Jonathan and Trientje Traphagen.

MYER, Jacob D. and Abigail—Annatje—Nov. 3.
Wit: Abel and Annatje Riddenaar.

CHRISTIE, Andries and Abigail—Antje, b. Nov. 3—Dec. 22.
Wit: Willem and Antje Hoppe.

1772

ZABRISKE, Hendrik C. and Maria—Abram—Jan. 2.
Wit: Petrus A. and Catrina Haring.

ACKERMAN, David D. and Jannetje—Aaltje—June 9.
Wit: Jacobus and Tittie Pilesfelt.

ALYEE, Albert and Maria—Albert—June 28.
Wit: Albert and Rachel Hoppe.

POST, Isaac and Jannetje—Abram—Sept. 6.
Wit: Abram and Sara Post.

MARIE, Jan and Lea—Abram—Dec. 6.
Wit: Abram W. and Grietje Rutan.

TRAPHAGEN, Jonathan and Trientje—Annatje, b. Nov. 2—Dec. 6.

DOBBS, William and Rachel—Abigael, Dec. 6.

1773

VAN VOORHEESE, Jan W. and Lea—Albert and Jacobus (twins)—Feb. 21.
Wit: Albert W. and Jannitje Van Voorhees; Petrus J. and Marietje
Van Blerkom.
TOIRS, Laurens and Lisabeth—Annaatje—Mar. 7.
Wit: Arie and Annatje Vanderbeek.
HERRING, Jan D. and Lisabeth—Ariaantje, b. Feb. 22—Mar. 21.
CHRISTIE, James and Bethsie—Antje—Apr. 11.
Wit: Abram and Marytje Ackerman.
GARDENIER, Hans and Jacomyntje—Annatje—June 6.
Wit: Abram and Annatje Banta.
TERHUYN, Steven D. and Jannetje—Albert—June 6.
Wit: Albert C. and Aaltje Zabriske.
ZABRISKE, Abram and Marietje—Albert—July 11.
Wit: Albert H. and Jannitje A. Zabriske.
TERHUYN, Abram and Marytje—Abraham—Aug. 29.
Wit: Hannes and Antje Westervelt.

1774

BANTA, Jacob A. and Rachel—Annatje—Jan. 3.
Wit: Abram and Annatje Banta.
DUBOUW, Pieter A. and Gerrebrecht—Andries—Jan. 23.
Wit: Andries and Jannitje Dubow.
TERHUYN, Samuel and Lea—Albert—Apr. 29.
Wit: Albert and Sara Terhuyn.
POST, Abram and Jannitje—Annaatje—Sept. 4.
Pieter and Annatje Jersie.
SMITH, Willem and Grietje—Annatje—Sept. 12.
Wit: Frans Smith; Annatje Dumaree.
HOPPE, Andries and Maria—Antje—Oct. 9.
Wit: Abram G. and Lea Gerritse.
WARENT, John and Elisabeth—Antje—Nov. 6.
Wit: Cornelis and Lisabeth Ackerman.
HELM, Samuel and Trina—Annatje, b. Nov. 31—Dec. 18.
Wit: Benjamin and Annatje Zabriske.

1775

VANDERBEEK, Abram J. and Susanna—Abraham—Jan. 22.
Wit: Hannes and Abigael Vanderbeek.
VANGELDER, Cobus and Jannitje—Annatje, b. Jan. 30—Feb. 19.
Wit: Abram D. and Annatje Ackerman.
V[AN] BLERKOM, Devid J. and Gerritje—Abram—Mar. 12.
Wit: Jan and Lea Maybe.
BOGERT, Steven and Geesje—Angonietje—Apr. 23.
Wit: David J. and Antje Ackerman.
BOGERT, Joost C. and Marietje—Aaltje—May 14.
Wit: Jan I. and Lea Zabriske.
VANHOREN, Cornelis C. and Geesje—Adam, b. Aug. 14—Sept. 10.
Wit: Adam and Grietje Van Orden.
BONGERT, Andries and Trientje—Andries—Oct. 1.
Wit: Cristiaan I. and Marietje Zobriskie.

STEGG, Isaac and Lena—Angonietje—Oct. 22.
Wit: David J. and Antje Ackerman.

ZABRISKE, Joost C. and Polly—Antje—Dec. 26.
Wit: Jan A. and Antje G. Hoppe.

1776

ZOBRISKE, Jacob H. and Wyntje—Abraham—Jan. 14.
Wit: Albert A. Terhuyn; Marietje I. Zobriske.

VAN GELDER, Hendrik and Antje—Antje—Feb. 4.
Wit: Abram and Grietje Van Voorhese.

RIDNAER, Coenraad and Elisabeth—Abel, b. Jan. 28—Feb. 18.
Wit: Abel and Susanna Ridnaer.

MEYER, Martin J. and Gerrebrecht—Aaltje, b. Feb. 19—Mar. 9.
Wit: Hannes D. and Aaltje Ackerman.

VAN VOORHESE, Isaac L. and Pryntje—Albert, b. Feb. 19—Mar. 17.
Wit: Albert and Rachel Ackerman.

HOPPE, Gerret H. and Antje—Andries—Apr. 21.
Wit: Jan J. and Lea Zabriske.

BOGERT, Cobus J. and Cornelia—Angonietje—May 5.
Wit: David H. and Antje Ackerman.

HOPPE, Abram H. and Antje—Antje—June 16.
Wit: Jan J. and Lea Zabriske.

DEGROOT, David and Elsje—Angonietje—Aug. 25.
Wit: Isaac and Syntje Dey.

LUTKENS, Jan and Grietje—Antje—Sept. 15.
Wit: Cornelis and Sara Vandien.

DOREMES, Hannis and Jannitje—Andries, b. Sept. 4—Oct. 6.
Wit: Andries A. and Annatje Van Boskerk.

POST, Jacob and Saartje—Abram, b. Sept. 11—Oct. 6.
Wit: Abram and Jannitje Post.

HOPPE, Jonathan and Grietje—Albert—Oct. 6.
Wit: Albert and Rachel Hoppe.

1778

TERHUYN, Steve D. and Jannitje—Albert—Aug. 2.
Wit: Jan J. and Lea Zabriske.

VAN BLERCUM, Pieter and Jannitje—Antje, b. Dec. 9—Dec. 20.
Wit: Isaac and Antje Bogert.

1779

VAN BLERCOM, Lena—Antje—Sept. 2.
Wit: William and Grietje Smith.

ZABRISKIE, Christian and Martyntje—Andries—Dec. 24.
Wit: Andries and Lisabeth Zabriskie.

1780

VAN ORDER, Jannitje—Abel—Apr. 9.
Wit: David and Pollie Van Blercom.

PULISFELT, Andries—Andries—Apr. 8.

ACKERMAN, David G. and Aaltje—Albert—Nov. 19.
Wit: Albert and Lisabeth Terhuyn.

1781

ZABRISKIE, Albert J. and Matje—Aaltje—Sept. 2.
Wit: Abraham H. and Antje Hopper.

HOPPER, Jan H. and Fytje—Annetje—Sept. 2.
Wit: Hendrik and Margriet Doremus.

VALENTYNE, Jacob and Grietje—Abraham—Nov. 1.

VAN BLERCOM, Hannes and Rebecca—Albert—Nov. 10.
Wit: Albert W. and Jannitje Van Voorhese.

1782

V[AN] BOSKERCK, Thomas A. and Maria—Annatje—Feb. 17.

1783

VAN HOORN, Cornelis—Andois—Feb. 16.

1782

ZABRISKE, Andries and Carstina—Aaltje—Dec. 11.
Wit: Albert and Geesje Zabriske.

1783?

VAN BEECK, Arie—Annatje—Aug. 25.
Wit: Jacobus Bogert and wife.

HOPPE, Gerrit—Albert—Sept. 1.
Wit: Albert and Rachel Banta.

1783

LUTKENS, Harmen—Antje—Sept. 7.
Wit: Jan Vandebeek and wife.

ACKERMAN, Jan—Antje—Dec. 7.
Wit: Johannis Ratan and wife.

WILSEN, Albert—Antje—Dec. 15.
Wit: Abraham Hoppe and wife.

1784

VAN BLERCOM, Pieter—Andries—Aug. 8.

TERHUNE, Steven and Jannitje—Annatje—Aug. 22.
Wit: David and Annatje Terhune.

HOPPE, Abraham—Andries—Aug. 22.
Wit: Andries Hoppe and wife.

1785

MEYER, Marte—Abraham—Jan. 1.

VAN BLERCOM, Pieter—Annatje—Feb. 20.
Wit: Lewis Meltenberrie and wife.

POST, Pieter—Abram—Mar. 20.
Wit: Laurens Van Orden and wife.

McPHERSON, Abraham and Jennie—Antje, b. Apr. 15—May 22.

1786

GERRITSE, Johannis and Maria—Albert, b. Mar. 26—Apr. 16.
Wit: Wyntje Zabriske.

HOPPE, Hendrik and Jacomyntje—Andreas, b. Aug. 5—Sept. 10.
Wit: Pieter and Antje Hoppe.

1789

BERTOLF, Jacobus and Lea—Abraham, b. Feb. 10—Mar. 1.
Wit: Abraham and Grietje Rotan.

HÖPPE, Isaac and Rachel—Albert, b. Feb. 14—Mar. 15.

HOPPE, Gerrit J. and Maria—Arie, b. Feb. 26—Mar. 22.

VAN BLERCOM, Johannis and Rebecka—Annaatje, b. Mar. 2—Apr. 4.
Wit: William and Annaatje Van Voorhesen.

WOERTENDYK, Cornelis and Sophia—Abraham, b. July 3—July 19.

ACKERMAN, Arie and Christina—Aart Cuyper, b. Aug. 2—Aug. 23.

1790

VAN BOSKERK, Jan and Sara—Annaatje, b. Dec. 12, 1789—Jan. 24.
Wit: Jacob and Annaatje Servent.

VAN HOORN, Daniel and Annatje—Antje—Jan. 31.
Wit: Pieter and Antje Demarest.

MESSEKER, Lodewyk and Sara—Abraham—Mar. 14.

DURIE, Petrus and Osseltje—Annatje, b. Feb. 13—Mar. 15.
Wit: Daniel and Annatje Demarest.

HOPPE, Hendrik G. and Rachel—Albert, b. June 12—Aug. 4.
Wit: Albert G. and Rachel Hoppe.

ECKERSON, Edward and Catrina—Angonietje, b. May 18—Aug. —.
Wit: David and Angenietje Eckerson.

FESYUER, Abraham and Elisabeth—Annatje—Oct. —.

DEBAEN, Petrus and Maria—Angonietje, b. Sept. 6—Oct. –
Wit: David and Angonietje Eckerson.

GERRITSEN, Johannis and Maria—Antje, b. Dec. 1—Dec. 5.
Wit: Abraham and Antje Hoppe.

1791

SNYDER, Jacob and Grietje—Adam, b. Dec. 13, 1790—Jan. 3.

VANDERBEEK, Coenradus and Annaatje—Angenietje, b. Dec. 15, 1790.
Jan. 3.
Wit: Jurrie and Maria Vanderbeek.

BANTA, Hendrik and Margrietje—Angenietje, b. Jan. 2—Feb. —.
Wit: Jacob and Hester Banta.

ACKERMAN, David and Jannitje—Abraham, b. Feb. 6—Feb. 24.?
Wit: Abraham and Maria Blauvelt.

ZABRISKIE, Christiaan A. and Maria—Abraham, b. May 3.

VENDERBECK, Jan and Aaltje—Abraham, b. May 27.
Wit: Abraham H. and Antje Hoppe.

SMYTH, John and Sara—Antje, b. Apr. 10—June 29.
Wit: David and Jacomyntje Ackerman.

SCHUYLER, Adonia and Elisabeth—Arend, b. Apr. 26—June 12.

HOPPE, Jan J. and Catrina—Antje, b. July 12—Aug. 4.
Wit: Gerrit H. and Antje Hoppe.

ECKERSON, Edward P. and Hetty—Annatje, b. July 29—Aug. 21.
Wit: Jacob and Annatje Servent.

Bos, Pieter and Frone—Annatje, b. Aug. 27—Oct. 2.
Wit: Edward P. and Hette Eckerson.

1786

JANSE, Abraham and Elisabeth—Aaltje, b. Sept. 23—Oct. —.
Wit: Cornelis and Sara Van Hoorn.

V[AN] BLERKOM, Johannis and Rebecka—Abigail, b. Sept. 15—Oct. 8.

1787

BLAUVELT, Abraham and Margrietje—Abraham, b. July 9, 1786—Jan. 2.
DEBOW, Andreas and Francyntje—Abraham, b. Oct. 6.
Wit: Hendrik and Jannitje Terhuun.
HORN, Joseph and Maria—Andreas, b. Jan. 17—Mar. 4.
Wit: Andreas and Catrina Hoppe.
BOGERT, Albert I. and Maria—Aaltje, b. Jan. 27—Mar. 11.
Wit: Hendrik and Aaltje Storm.
WRITE, Albert and Geertje—Aaltje—Aaltje, b. May 28—June 21.
Wit: Jan J. and Lea Zabriskie.
ZABRISKE, Abraham and Maria—Aaltje, b. July 3—July 15.
Wit: David G. and Aaltje Ackerman.
HOPPE, Hendrik G. and Rachel—Aaltje, b. Aug. 14—Sept. 9.
Wit: Abraham and Antje Hoppe.
DEBOW, Pieter and Susanna—Annatje—Oct. 28.
Wit: William and Annatje Van Voorhesen.

1788

HOPPE, Gerrit I. and Maria—Abraham—Feb. 3.
Wit: Abraham I. and Geertje Hoppe.
BERTOLF, Samuel and Elsje—Albert—Feb. 3.
ECKERSON, Thomas and Susanna—Angenietje, b. Jan. 4—Feb. 3.
Wit: David and Angenietje Eckerson.
VAN HOORN, Cornelis B. and Sara—Antje, b. Apr. 1—Apr. 20.
Wit: David and Antje Ackerman.
SMITH, Albert and Susanna—Albert, b. Mar. 15—Apr. 20.
HOPPE, Petrus and Elisabeth—Albert—May 4.
BROWER, Petrus and Rachel—Abraham, b. June 8—June 22.
Wit: Johannes and Annatje Ackerman.
CUYPER, Hendrik and Antje—Andrew—July 20.
Wit: Andrew and Maritje Van Orden.
BROWN, James and Anna—Anna—July 20.
VAN RYPEN, Johannis and Geertje—Antje, b. Sept. 13—Sept. 28.
Wit: Gerrit and Abigail Van Rypen.
MEBIE, Isaac and Sara—Abraham, b. Sept. 19—Oct. 19.
Wit: Jacob and Sara Post.
ACKERMAN, Johannis and Elisabeth—Annatje—Nov. 16.
Wit: Jacobus and Annatje Perry.
JANSE, Abraham and Elisabeth—Abraham, b. Dec. 6—Dec. 21.
Wit: Abraham and Maria Blauvelt.

1789

VANDERBEEK, Jacob and Maria—Abraham, b. Dec. 16, 1788—Jan. 18.
Wit: Abraham and Jannetje Vanderbeek.
SMIT, Abraham and Grietje—Aaltje, b. Oct. 17, 1788—Jan. 18.
Wit: Arie and Aaltje Blauvelt.
ACKERMAN, John and Annatje—Abraham, b. Jan. 4—Jan. 29.
Wit: Petrus and Rachel Brower.
VANDERBEEK, Cornelis and Hilletje—Abram, b. Sept. 12—Oct. 9.
Wit: Abraham and Susanna Vanderbeek.

1792

ZABRISKE, Abraham and Maria—Abraham, b. Feb. 17—Feb. 26.
Wit: Albert and Aaltje Terhuen.

ZABRISKE, Albert and Metje—Albert, b. Mar. 25—Apr. 10.

ECKERSON, Thomas and Susanna—Annatje, b. Mar. 25—June 16.
Wit: Abraham and Annaatje Lesyer.

DEBAEN, Joost—Antje, b. May 27—June 16.
Wit: Jacob and Antje Debaen.

FOLLE, Willem and Antje—Adam, b. May 29—June 16.
Wit: Thomas and Hester Stag.

VANDERBEEK, Arie and Lena—Angenietje, b. Apr. 24—June 21.

BROUWER, Petrus and Rachel—Antje—Nov. 11.
Wit: Harman and Antje Vanderbeek.

1793

BOGERT, Albert and Maria—Abraham, b. Oct. 18, 1792—Feb. 10.

ACKERMAN, Jacobus and Annatje—Abraham, b. Mar. 8—Mar. 31.
Wit: Paulus and Rachel Vanboskerk.

VAN IMBURG, Hendrik and Maria—Albert, b. June 25—Jul 7
Wit: Albert and Maritje Van Voorhesen.

McCALL, John and Geertrui—Archibald, b. Apr. 28—July 7.

VAN VOORHESEN, Jan and Tryntje—Abraham—Aug. 4.
Wit: Jacobus and Maria Ackerman.

VANDEVOTE, Paul and Elisabeth—Abraham, b. July 10—Aug. 4.
Wit: John and Lena Romyn.

POOST, John and Annatje—Abraham and Elisabeth (twins), b. Aug. 26—
Sept. 22.
Wit: Isaak and Sara Mebe.

CAMPBELL, John and Jane—Archibold, b. Aug. 28—Sept. 15.

HORN, Jacob and Femmetje—Abraham, b. Sept. 11—Oct. 20.
Wit: Johannes and Jannitje Dremus.

DEBAEN, Petrus and Maria—Antje, b. Oct. 23—Nov. 17.
Wit: Jacob and Antje Debaan.

BOS, Dirk and Antje—Antje, b. Nov. 22—Dec. 15.
Wit: Lodewyck and Leentje Bos.

1794

HOPPE, Stephen and Geertje—Abraham, b. Jan. 6—Jan. 19.
Wit: Albert and Aaltje Terhune.

WESTERVELT, Abraham and Antje—Abraham, b. Jan. 6—Jan. 14.

POTTER, John and Maria—Adam, b. Jan. 7.—Jan. 26.

ACKERMAN, David and Aaltje—Abraham, b. Jan. 30—Feb. 9.
Wit: Abraham and Margrietje Rotan.

ACKERMAN, Abraham and Elisabeth—Albert, b. Jan. 10—Feb. 9.
Wit: Johannis and Lena Pecker.

ACKERMAN, Jacobus G. and Rachel—Annatje, b. Jan. 28—Feb. 23.
Wit: Cornelis and Hester Van Saan.

WOERTENDYK, Albert and Grietje—Abraham, b. Feb. 16—Mar. 16.
Wit: Abraham and Lea Debaan.

VAN ORDEN, Thomas and Lea—Aaltje, b. Feb. 13—Mar. 20.
Wit: David D. and Metje Ackerman.

WOERTENDYK, Cornelius and Sophia—Abraham, b. Apr. 17—May 18.
HOPPE, Hendrik and Aaltje—Aaltje, b. June 29—July 27.
Wit: Andrias and Elisabeth Hoppe.
VAN RYPEN, Johannis and Geertje—Adriaan, b. July 9—July 27.
Wit: Abraham and Catrina Cadmus.
BLAUVELT, Frederick and Elisabeth—Aaltje, b. July 30—Aug. 31.
Wit: Aaltje Blauvelt.
RIDDENAAR, John and Catrina Van Houten—Abel, b. Mar. 14—Aug. 31.
V[AN]D BEEK, Cornelis and Hilletje—Andreas, b. Sept. 23—Oct. 26.
FESJEUR, Abraham and Elisabeth—Abraham, b. Sept. 25—Nov. 2.
BOGERT, Casparus and Jannitje—Andreas, b. Oct. 8—Nov. 9.
Wit: Christiaan and Maria Zabriske.
ZABRISKE, Jan and Jannetje—Andreas, b. Nov. 1—Nov. 23.
Wit: Andreas and Christina Zabriske.
VAN RYPE, Frederick and Maria—Angenietje, b. Oct. 1—Nov. 23.
Wit: Maria V. d. Beek.

1795

ACKERMAN, Johannis and Annatje—Arie, b. Dec. 27, 1794—Feb. 11.
Wit: David and Metje Ackerman.
VANHOORN, John and Elisabeth—Abraham, b. Jan. 31—Feb. 19.
Wit: Abraham and Geertje Hoppe.
ACKERMAN, Gerrit and Geertje—Aaltje, b. Feb. 15—Mar. 5.
Wit: David and Aaltje Ackerman.
TERHUNE, Jacob and Maria—Abraham, Feb. 22—Mar. 15.
Wit: Abraham Terhune.
WRIGHT, John and Abigail—Aaltje, b. May 18—June 28.
Wit: Cornelis and Aaltje Bogert.
Bos, Dirk and Antje—Antje, b. July 11—July 19.
Wit: Lodewyk and Leentje Bos.
TERHUNE, Albert and Aaltje—Abraham, b. July 4—Aug. 9.
Wit: Hendrik and Rachel Terhune.
VAN KLEEFT, Joseph and Elisabeth—Abraham, b. Aug. 5—Sept. 20.
BEYERD, David and Grietje—Adam—Oct. 18.
Wit: Coenraad and Maria Wannemaker.
WOERTENDYCK, Reinier and Annaatje—Abraham, b. Nov. 3—Nov. 22.
Wit: Abraham and Elisabeth Fesjeur.
ACKERMAN, Johannis and Maria—Angenietje, b. Oct. 27—Nov. 22.

1796

ACKERMAN, Daniel and Cathalyntje—Annatje, b. Jan. 6—Jan. 24.
Wit: John and Annaatje Christe.
VANDERBEEK, Coenraad and Annatje—Angenietje, b. Mar. 3—Mar. 27.
LESIER, Abraham and Annaatje—Angenietje and Maria, b. Jan. 18—Mar. 28.
Wit: David and Angenietje Eckersen; Petrus and Maria Debaan.
MASSEKER, Dirk and Lena—Aaltje, b. Dec. 8, 1795—Apr. 3.
ROTAN, Jan and Rachel—Abram, b. July 4—Aug. 7.
Wit: Abraham and Susanna V. d. Beek.
DECKER, Cornelius and Lea—Antje, b. June 4—Aug. 7.
Wit: Elizabeth Carlough.

DOREMUS, Andries and Abigael—Annaatje, b. Sept. 11—Sept. 25.
Wit: Johannes and Jannetje Doremus.
BROUWER, John and Catrina—Abraham, b. Nov. 9—Dec. 25.
TERHUEN, Albert and Rachel—Abraham, b. Oct. 15.

1797
ZABRISKE, Albert and Metje—Antje, b. Jan. 17—Feb. 19.
WRIGHT, Abraham and Annatje—Aaltje, b. Mar. 25—Apr. 23.
HOPPE, Hendrik A. and Charity—Abraham, b. Apr. 26—May 21.
Wit: Abraham H. and Antje Hoppe.
ROTAN, Daniel and Jannetje—Abram, b. July 5—Aug. 20.
Wit: Abram and Angenietje Van Voorhesen.
DEBAEN, Jacob and Geesje—Annaatje, b. July 4—Sept. 2.
Wit: Thomas and Geertje Banta.
MEBE, Pieter and Jannitje—Annatje, b. Aug. 25—Sept. 2.
BANTA, Abraham and Dievertje—Abraham, b. Sept. 17—Dec. 24.

1798
RIDMAN, Abraham and Elisabeth—Abraham, b. Jan. 28—Feb. 11.
Wit: Gerritje Van Blercum.
HOPPE, Adries and Sara—Albert, b. Mar. 22—Apr. 15.
ACKERMAN, Gerrit and Geertje—Andreas, b. May 5—May 29.
DEBAEN, Petrus and Maria—Annaatje, b. May 17—June 3.
Wit: Abraham and Annatje Lesier.
FESYEUR, Abraham and Elisabeth—Antje, b. Jan. 27—June 20.
Wit: Jacob and Antje Debaan.
DURIE, John and Rachel—Annaatje, b. May 25—June 20.
POULISVELT, Pieter and Nansje—Annaatje, b. May 24—June 20.

1799
VAN BOSKERCK, Pieter and Selle—Abraham, b. Nov. 21, 1798—Apr. 14.
Wit: Abraham and Jennie Van Boskerck.
HEDDE, Jesaia and Elisabeth—Antje—Mar. 15.
Wit: Jose and Aaltje Poost.
ZABRISKE, Jacob and Elisabeth—Aaltje, b. Apr. 16—July 7.
Wit: Hendrik and Aaltje Hopper.
BOS, Lodewyk and Leentje—Andrias, b. May 6—July 7.
Wit: Andrias and Jannetje Debaan.
ACKERMAN, Daniel and Teyne—Antje, b. Aug. 24—Sept. 8.
Wit: Willem and Antje Christie.
ECKERSON, Paulus and Maria—Angenietje, b. Aug. 6—Oct. 6.
Wit: David and Angenietje Eckerson.
TERHUNE, John and Egje—Annatje, b. Sept. 25—Oct. 27.
Wit: Christiaan A. and Maria Zabriske.
ZABRISKE, Nicholas and Annatje—Annatje, b. Oct. 19—Nov. 10.
Wit: Benjamin and Annatje Zabriskie.
MORE, John and Jane—Anna, b. Oct. 23—Dec. 15.

1800
HOPPER, Andrew and Antie—Albert, b. Dec. 30, 1799—Jan. 23.
Wit: Albert and Marytje Van Voorhees.
BANTA, Thomas and Peggy—Antje, b. Oct. 10, 1799—Feb. 2.

ALYEA, Hendrik and Sara—Annatje, b. Mar. 25, 1799—Feb. 22.
ZABRISKIE, Albert and Aaltje—Albert, b. Jan. 11—Feb. 16.
VAN SCHYVEN, William and Saartje—Abraham, b. Feb. 20—Apr. 6.
Wit: John and Aaltje Debaen.
ZABRISKIE, Jacob and Wyntje—Aaltje, b. May 21—July 17.
Wit: Albert and Aaltje Terhune.
ACKERMAN, Gerrit and Geertje—Andreas, b. Aug. 7—Aug. 24.
LESIER, Abraham and Annatje—Abraham, b. Sept. 25—Nov. 30.

1753
Bos, Samuel and Rebecka—Benjamin—March 18.
Wit: Dom. Benj. and Lisabeth Vandelinde.

1768
VESEUR, Hannes and Lena—Barend—May 15.
Wit: Barend and Francyntje Veseur.

1770
QUACKENBOS, Hannes and Margrita—Barend—Feb. 25.
Wit: Klaas and Marietje Haledrom.

1771
DUMAREE, Daniel D. and Cornelia—Belitie—June 23.
Wit: Pieter and Belitie Outwater.

1772
ZABRISKE, Jacob J. and Jannitje—Belitie—Jan. 12.
Wit: Albert J. and Geesje Zabriske.

1773
PIETERIE, Willem and Santje—Barend, b. April 12—May 2.
AYCRIGG, John and Rachel—Benjamin—Oct. 10.
From the Parish of Upton upon Severn, Worcestershire O. England.
Wit: Albert A. Terhuyn and Lisabeth Leydecker.

1774
VERSEUR, Pieter and Maria—Barend, b. March 29—April 24.
Wit: Barent and Syntje Verseur.

1775
WESSELS, Joseph and Ariaantje—Benjamin—April 2.
Wit: Hannes Smith and wife.
GARDENIER, Johannis and Jacomyntje—Barend—April 17.
Wit: Barend and Francyntje Veseur.

1780
ZABRISKE, Jacob J. and Jannitje—Belitie—Oct. 15.
Wit Albert and Geesje Zabriske.

1785
ODEL, Gerrit and Rebecka—Benjamin—March 20.
Wit: Hendrik and Maria Odel.

1786
RYER, Jan and Maria—Barend, b. March 7—April 1.
Wit: Barent and Francyntje Fesyeur.

1788
MAURUSSEN, Nathaniel and Elisabeth—Brechje, b. Aug. 8—Aug. 31.

1789
SHURTE, Adolph and Elisabeth—Benjamin, b. Feb. 22—March 29.
Wit: Jacobus and Jannitje Demarest.

1790
RIGWAY, John and Grietje—Betsey—March 14.
DEBAAN, Jacob and Antje—Brechje, b. Feb. 19—March 15.
Wit: Abraham and Brechje Debaan.

BOS, Lodewyk and Leentje - Barend, b. May 7 - Aug. 3
Wit: Barend and Francyntje Fesyeur.

1791
JANSE, Abraham and Elisabeth - Barend, b. March 23 - April 24.
Wit: Daniel and Margrietje Ackerman.

1794
VAN WERT, Isaac and Elisabeth - Betsey, b. July 20 - Aug. 24.
Wit: David Paulisvelt and Bethsy Shoemaker.

1797
COLE, Adriaan and Elisabeth - Barend, b. June 30 - Aug. 20.

1749
WALLI, Elias and Anna - Claartje - Aug. 13.
Wit: Pieter and Claartje Wannemaker.

1750
MABE, Pieter and Rachel - Casparus - Feb. 4.
Wit: Casparus and Willempje Mebe.
DUREMUS, Abram and Annatje - Catrina, b. Jan. 22.
Wit: Samuel and Rebecka Bos.
STORM, Hendrik and Cornelia - Coenradus, b. March 26.
Wit: Coenradus and Angenietje Vanderbeek.
ZABRISKE, Albert and Aaltje - Cristiaan - Nov. 28.
Wit: Hendrik and Neesje Zabriske.

1751
ZABRISKIE, Andries and Lisabeth - Cristiaan - Feb. 24.
Wit: Albert and Aaltje Zabriske.
VAN BOSSE, Hermanus and Abigail - Catharine - Aug. 18.
Wit: Isaac and Janneke Kingsland.

DERYIE, Daniel and Vrouwtje—Catharina—Oct. 20.
Wit: Dirk and Catryntje Vandien.
SLINGERLAND, Teunis and Hendrika—Casparus—Oct. 27.
Wit: Hermanus and Jenneke Degrau.

1752

USTERLI, Marten and Grouda—Catrientje, b. Dec. 16, 1751—Jan. 19.
Wit: Pieter and Margrietje Dubou.
RIDDENAAR, Hendrik and Grietje-Coenraad-Jun 28.
Wit: Abram and Rachel Van Gelder.

1753

BALLDIN, Steven and Antje—Carstina—April 23.
Wit: Joost and Carstine Zabriske.
HOPPE, David—Cornelia—July 22.
Wit: Jan and Antje Bogert.

1754

KUYPER, Cornelis and Mettie—Catharina—Feb. 9.
Wit: Dirk and Tryntje Vandien.
VANDERBEEK, Jurrien and Marytje—Coenradus—March 10.
Wit: Paulus and Annatje Vanderbeek.
VOLLIK, Niklaas and Metje—Sara—Sept. 8.
Wit: Benjamin and Nellie Odel.
ZOBRISKE, Hendrik C. and Maria—Christiaan—Sept. 29.
Wit: Albert C. and Aaltje Zobriske.

1755

VAN RYPE, Fredrik and Antje—Cornelis, b. June 27—July 13.
Wit: Cornelis and Antje Van Vorst.

1756

DEGRAU, Hermanus and Jannike—Casparus—July 11.
Wit: Andries and Jannitie Debouw.

1758

VAN BLERCOM, Isaac and Sara—Cornelia—March 5.
Wit: Egbert and Sara Van Zeyl.
BONGAERT, Cornelis Y. and Elisabeth—Casparus—April 9.
Wit: Silvester and Mechtel Earl.

1760

FOCHI,[1] Barend and Francyntje—Catharina, b. June 24—Aug. 9.
Wit: Jan and Catharina Fochi.
MEYER, Hannes I. and Leentje—Cornelis—Aug. 5.
Wit: Hermanus and Aaltje V[an] Blercom.

1761

KOGH, Casper and Lidea—Casparus—Oct. 18.
Wit: Anna Maria and Elias Kogh.
BANTA, Jan Jo. and Sara—Catrientje, b. Nov. 17—Nov. 29.
Wit: Jan H. and Tryntje Banta.

---

[1] This Fochi is doubtless a corruption of Verschuur, Fresheur, etc.

1762

Lutkens, Harme and Antje—Catrientje—May 2.
Wit: Steven and Catryntje Zabriske.
Van Blerkom, Pieter and Sucke—Carstyntje—Oct. 24.
Wit: Jan and Carstyntje Ackerman.
Perry, Daniel and Jannitje—Catrina, b. Nov. 16—Dec. 12.
Wit: Jan and Catrina Voseur.
Quackenbush, Reinier and Catrina—Catrina, b. Nov. 15—Dec. 12.
Wit: Abram and Gerritje Quackinbush.
Van Zeyl, Pieter and Lena—Saartje—Nov. 12.
Wit: Egbert and Saartje Van Zeyl.

1764

Doremes, Hendrik and Aagje—Catrina, b. Jan. 24—Feb. 9.
Wit: Johannes and Pryntje Van Houten.
Caerlog, Hendrik and Grietje—Coenraad—July 8.
Wit: Coenraad and Antje Bruyn.

1765

Perry, Daniel and Jannitje—Catharina—Jan. 27.
Wit: Jan and Catrina Voseur.
Straet, Dirk and Rebecka—Catharina, b. Mar. 1—April 14.
Wit: Jacob and Sara Straet.
Magdanel, Cornelis and Catrina—Cornelis, b. April 7—May 5.
Wit: John J. and Maria Eckersen.
Pielesfelt, Coenraad and Eva—Cornelis and Petrus, (twins)—Nov. 3.
Wit: Cornelis and Cornelia Pielesfelt.

1766

Perry, Cobus and Annatje—Catrina—March 16.
Wit: Isaac and Maragriet Perry.
Voseur, Willem —————— —Cornelis—March 23.
Wit: Cornelis Blauvelt.
Nix, Hermanus —————— —Catrina—April 27.
Wit: Andries and Jannitje Debouw.
Mourusse, Jacobus and Lena—Catrina—June 22.
Wit: Pieter A. Debouw and Catrina Duremus.
Haring, —————— Lea—Christiana, b. May 21—June 29.
Wit: Cornelis and Catrina Haring.
Hoppe, Gerrit H. and Antje—Catryntje—May 9.
Wit: Hendrik and Claartje Traphage.

1767

Terhuyn, Steven D. and Jannitje—David—Nov 15.
Wit: David and Sara Terhuyn.

1768

Rutan, Cobus and Willampje—Saartje—Jan. 4.
Wit: Saartje and Abram Rutan.
Bogert, Jacobus and Cornelia—Cornelia—April 3.
Wit: David and Rachel Hoppe.
Jersey, Hendrik —————— —Catrina—Aug. 28.
Wit: Jacob and Maria Bogert.

Symesse, Walter and Rachel—Catrina—Oct. 7.
Davenpoort, Pieter and Lea—Catrina—Mar. 16.

1769

Pilisfelt, Willem and Elisabeth—Coenraad—Nov. 5.

1770

Verseur, Hannes and Lena—Cornelis, b. June 6—July 1.
  Wit: Cornelis A. and Maria Banta.
Syourt, Willem and Catrina—Christiaan—July 29.
Terhuyn, Steven D. and Jannitje—Christiaan—Sept. 30.
  Wit: Christiaan A. and Martyntje Zabriskie.

1771

Vandien, Gerrit and Sara—Cornelis—Feb. 24.
  Wit: Thomas and Polly Vandien.
Blauvelt, David and Rachel—Cornelis, b. Jan. 25—Feb. 24.
  Wit: Willem and Lisabeth Verseur.
Baeldin, Steven and Antje—Cristina, b. Apr. 6, 1756—Feb. 24.
Helm, Samuel and Catrina—Cornelis, b. July 6—July 21.
  Wit: Cornelis and Grietje Helm.

1772

Zabriske, Joost and Marytje—Casparus—July 19.
  Wit: John T. Earl and Antje Baldwin.
Van Blerkom, Frans and Jacomyntje—Cornelis—Oct. 25.
  Wit: Pieter H. and Jannetje Van Blerkom.
Carns, Duglas and Geesje—Cornelia—Sept. 6.
  Wit: David Carns and Rachel Van Horen.

1773

Bogert, Joost and Marietje—Cornelis—Jan. 10.
  Wit: Cornelis and Elisabeth Bogert.
Van Blerkom, Pieter H. and Jannitje—Cornelis—May 16.
  Wit: Frans and Jacomyntje Van Blerkom.

1774

Coel, Jacob J. and Geertrui—Catrina, b. Jan. 30—June 28.
  Wit: Joannes and Catrina Coel.
Ryker, Pieter and Lea—Cornelis, b. Feb. 28, 1773—June 28.

1775

Miltenberry, Luwes and Lisabeth—Crastina—July 2.
Van Boskerck, Joost and Marytje—Cornelia—July 9.
  Wit: Willem and Cornelia Verburgh.
Pulles, Hendrik and Cathalyntje—Cornelis, b. Aug. 9—Sept. 10.
  Wit: Christiaan and Claartje Pulles.

1776

Zabriske, Hendrik I. and Willempje—Cornelis—July 14.

1782

Smith, Jacob and Rachel—Catrina, b. Apr. 8—Nov. 3.
  Wit: Albert J. and Annatje Bogert.

1780

Meyer, Andrew and Pegge—Cornelia—May 16.
  Wit: Cornelis and Cornelia Meyer.

1784

ZABRISKE, Christiaan and Marytje—Cornelis—April 25.

BERKHOF, Hendrik and Maria—Catrina, b. March 13—May 22.
Wit: Jan and Catrina Rose.

BLAUVELT, Cornelis and Catrina—Cathalyntje, b. Nov. 8—Dec. 5.
Wit: Christaan and Cathalyntje Blauvelt.

1785

DEBAAN, Joost and Margrietje—Catrina, b. Dec. 7—Dec. 11.
Wit: Jan and Elisabeth Debaan.

1787

FRERIKSE, Coenraad and Elisabeth—Catrina, b. Dec. 30, 1786—Aug. 9.
Wit: Robert and Catrina Frerikse.

ODEL, Gerrit and Rebecka—Catrina, b. May 6—May 27.

FERSYEUR, Jan W. and Wyntje—Catrientje, b. June 21—July 15.
Wit: Cornelis and Trientje Fersyeur.

1788

BERTOLF, Jillis and Sally—Catriena, b. Dec. 15, 1787—Jan. 20.
Wit: Christiaan A. and Marytje A. Zabriske.

HALDEROM, Cornelius and Margrietje—Catriena, b. Jan. 31—Feb.
Wit: Steven T. Bogert and Elisabeth Krom.

HENNION, William and Eva—Cornelis—April 27.

MICHLER, Lodewyk and Antje—Catriena—July 13.
Wit: Catriena Hofman.

VAN HOORN, Jacobus and Lea—Cornelis—Nov. 23.
Wit: Daniel and Annaatje Van Hoorn.

BOGERT, Casparus and Jannitje—Cornelis, b. Nov. 7—Nov. 30.
Wit: Joost and Maria Bogert.

1789

PULISFELT, Jan and Elisabeth—Coenraad, b. Dec. 10, 1788—Jan. 1.

GOETSCHIUS, Piatus and Catriena—Catriena, b. June 1—July 19.

BERTOLF, Jan and Susanna—Catriena, b. June 19—Aug. 9.
Wit: Hendrik and Marytje Storm.

STORM, Staats and Margrietje—Cornelia, b. Oct. 6—Oct. 25.
Wit: Hendrik and Cornelia Storm.

1790

POTTER, John and Maria—Caty—Aug. 15.
Wit: Thomas and Polly Snyder.

KOGH, Casparus C. and Margrietje—Casparus—Oct. 17.
Wit: Sara Kogh.

HOPPE, Petrus and Elisabeth—Cornelis, b. Nov. 9—Dec. 12.

KING, William and Myntje—Catriena, b. Nov. 21—Dec. 25.
Wit: Jan and Leentje Eckerson.

1791

HORN, Joseph and Maria—Catrina, b. July 10—Aug. 9.

1793

WESTERVELT, Albert C. and Maria—Cornelius, b. June 12—June 23.

SERVENT, Jacobus and Polly—Catrina, b. May 9—June 16.
Wit: Martyntje Van Boskerk.

SMITH, Gerrit and Hetty—Cornelius, b. Nov. 2—Nov. 17.
Wit: Cornelius and Becke Blauvelt.

1794

BERVOORT, Samuel and Martyntje—Christiaan, b. Feb. 19—March 20.
Wit: Christiaan J. and Maria Zabriskie.

Bos, Hendrik and Maritje—Coenraad, b. March 10—March 30.
Wit: Pieter Van Vlerkom and Elizabeth Bos.

AUSBON, John and Martyntje—Catriena and David (twins) b. Mar. 27
—March 30.
Wit: David Ausbon and Maria Van Boskerk.

ACKERMAN, Johannis and Elisabeth—Cornelius, b. June 8—July 6.
Wit: Cornelis and Maria Demarest.

ACKERMAN, Jacobus and Maria—Cornelia, b. July 12—Aug. 3.
Wit: Jacobus and Cornelia Bogert.

ACKERMAN, Petrus and Maria—Catriena, b. May 26—Aug. 24.
Wit: Joseph and Catriena Blauvelt.

MEYER, Marten and Brechje—Cornelis, b. Sept. 24—Nov. 9.

WANNEMAKER, Abraham and Annatje—Catriena, b. Dec. 1—Dec. 25.
Wit: Lourens and Maria Van Boskerk.

1795

SCHUYLER, Adonia and Elisabeth—Cornelis, b. April 30—June 14.
Wit: Andreas and Christina Zabriske.

VAN BLERCOM, John and Geertje—Catriena, b. July 13—Aug. 2.
Wit: Steven and Claartje Campbel.

VEIL, Enos and Nellie—Catharina, b. Aug. 24—Sept. 20.

TAALMAN, John and Margrietje—Catriena, b. Sept. 15—Oct. 25.

DODS, James and Maria—Catriena, b. Oct. 14—Nov. 22.

YOOMENS, John and Catriena—Coenraad, b. Nov. 3—Nov. 22.

1796

DEMAREST, David and Geesje—Cornelis, b. Dec. 7, 1795—Jan. 31.
Wit: Cornelis and Elisabeth Demarest.

PERRY, John and Charity—Cecilia, b. Oct. 26, 1795—March 13.

POULISVELT, Pieter and Nancy—Cornelia, b. Feb. 4—March 6.

POST, Gerrit A. and Nelly—Cornelis, b. March 11—March 27.

PECKER, William and Sally—Catriena, b. Aug. 2—Sept. 18.

SJOERT, Adolph and Aaltje—Catriena, b. Sept. 19—Sept. 25.
Wit: John and Catriena Youmens.

1797

ECKERSON, Cornelius and Catriena—Catriena, b. April 8—June 4.

HOPPE, Abraham and Elisabeth—Cornelius, b. Aug. 2—Aug. 20.
Wit: Jan G. and Rachel Hoppe.

1798

ZABRISKE, Jacob C. and Elisabeth—Christiaan, b. Jan. 6—Feb. 5.
Wit: Christiaan and Maria Zabriske.

CROUTER, Jacob and Maria—Cornelia, b. April 25—June 3.
Wit: Thomas and Cornelia Eckerson.

WESTERVELT, Petrus and Martyntje—Casparus, b. Aug. 21—Sept. 9.

1799

RIDDENAAR, Hendrick and Sally—Coen, b. July 6—July 21.

ACKERMAN, David and Metje—Catriena, b. Aug. 18—Sept. 1.

HALDEROM, William and Catriena—Catriena, b. Sept. 16—Oct. 6.
Wit: Andries and Catriena Halderom.

1800

DEBAAN, Andries and Jannitje—Catriena, b. Feb. 8—Feb. 23.
Wit: Samuel and Catriena Durie.

WESTERVELT, Albert and Maria—Casparus, b. April 5—April 10.

VAN BLERCOM, John and Geertje—Catriena, b. April 21—May 11.

WILLS, Thomas and Rachel—Catharina, b. June 14—June 29.
Wit: John Marinus and Jane Ackerman.

RIDDENAAR, Coenraad and Elisabeth—Catriena, b. July 13—Aug. 10.

STORM, Hendrik and Margrietje—Cornelius, b. July 28—Aug. 17.
Wit: Cornelius and Margrietje Halderom.

VANHORN, John and Elisabeth—Cornelius, b. Aug. 18—Sept. 7.

1750

WANNEMAKER, Christiaan and Grietje—Dirk—Jan. 21.
Wit: Pieter D. and Marytje Wannemaker.

1751

DUREMUS, Cornelius and Rachel—David—March 24.
Wit: Thomas and Marytje Ecker.

1753

JURRIXSE, Cobus and Rachel—David—Jan. 21.
Wit: David and Grietje Ackerman.

1754

VAN ZEYL, Petrus and Jannitje—Divertje—July 28.
Wit: Gerrit and Eva Bense.

1755

DUMAREST, Jacob and Rachel—Daniel, b. June 23—Aug. 17.
Wit: Samuel and Marytje Ecker.

VAN VOORHEES, Jan W. and Lea—Daniel—Aug. 21.
Wit: Daniel D. and Susanna Rutan.

RUTAN, William and Marytje—David—Dec. 14.
Wit: Abram J. and Hester Ackerman.

1756

RUTAN, Johannes and Aaltje—Daniel—April 15.
Wit: Albert and Antje V[an] Voorhees.

ACKERMAN, Niklaas and Maria—Daniel—May 9.
Wit: David Demarest and Fytje D. Westervelt.

1758
CROOFOOT, Elias—Deborah—May 13.
Wit: David Rensford.

1760
DERYIE, David and Vrouwtje—Dirk—Aug. 24.
Wit: Tryntje and Thomas Vandien.

1761
ALYEE, Isaac and Annaatje—David, b. Aug. 28—Nov. 29.
Wit: David and Agnietje Eckersen.

1762
SMITH, Daniel and Nansje—Dunken—Sept. 11.
VANHOREN, Lucas and Grietje—Daniel—Oct. 25.

1765
ACKERMAN, David A. and Jacomyntje—David—Jan. 27.
Wit: Jacobus and Cornelia Bongaart.

1766
ALYIE, Isaac and Annatje—David, b. Feb. 4—Feb. 23.
BOGERT, Margrietje—Dirk Wannemaker, b. Dec. 9, 1765—May 8.
Wit: Pieter and Rachel Bogert.

1768
STEGG, Cornelis and Grietje—David—May 1.
Wit: Guliam and Santje Dumaree.
MACKENNEL, Cornelis and Trientje—Daniel, b. June 22—June 24.
Wit: Philip and Sara Eckersen.
VANDIEN. Thomas and Polly—Dirk—Dec. 22.
Wit: Cornelis and Tryntje Vandien.

1769
V[AN] VOORHEESE, Jan. W. and Lea—Daniel—Feb. 5.
Wit: Abraham and Saartje Rutan.
WOERTENDYK, Frederik and Maseri—Divertje, b. Jan. 21—Feb. 9.
Wit: Jacob and Maria Woertendyk.
PERRY, Daniel and Jannitje—Daniel, b. Feb. 18—March 19.
Wit: Jan and Lisabeth Perry.
WESTERVELT, Johannis and Elisabeth—Dorothea—Sept. 10.
Wit: Cornelis L. and Elisabeth Bogert.
ACKERMAN, Willem and Grietje—Davidt—Dec. 24.
Wit: David J. and Antje Ackerman.

1770?
CHRISTIE, Andries and Abigail—David—March 18.
Wit: David and Wybrech Christe.
VESEUR, Willim and Lisabeth—David, b. Aug. 29—Sept. 9.
Wit: David and Rachel Blauvelt.

1770
ACKERMAN, David D. and Jannitje—Daniel (or David?)—Nov. 4.
Wit: Johannis Blauvelt.

1771
BLINKERHOF, Dirk S. and Osseltje—Dirk—Jan. 13.
BLAUVELT, Johannis and Catriena—David, b. Dec. 26, 1770—Feb. 3.

Post, Cobus and Mettie—David—Aug. 4.
Wit: Jacob S. and Vrouwtje Van Winkel.

1772

Dumaree, Pieter D. and Marytje—David—Jan. 12.
Wit: David and Sara Terhuyn.
Van Gelder, Hendrik and Antje—David—Sept. 13.
Wit: David and Wybrecht Christie.

1773

Berdan, Jacob D. and Sara—Dirk, b. Nov. 24—Dec. 19.
Wit: Lea Van Wageninge.

1774

Asley, John and Elisabeth—David—May 29.
Wit: David J. and Antje Ackerman.

1775

Blauvelt, Abram and Maria—Daniel—Jan. 8.
Wit: Gerrit and Tryntje Blauvelt.
Carns, Duglas and Geesje—Dorothie—April 24.
Vandien, Cornelis and Sara—Dirk—July 20.
Wit: Andries and Catharyntje Vandien.

1767

Terhune, Steven D.—David—Nov. 15.
Wit: David and Sara Terhune.

1775

Pulisvelt, Willem and Lisabeth—David, b. Aug. 5—Sept. 10.
Wit: Pieter Pulisvelt and Widow Coenraad Roiger.
Van Orden, Jan P. and Jannitje—David—Dec. 10.
Wit: David H. and Polly Van Blerkom.

1776

Hoppe, Hendrik I. and Aaltje—Dirk—June 16.
Wit: Hendrik D. and Polly Terhuyn.

1778

Bos, Samuel, Jr., and Lena—David—Nov. 15.
Wit: Pieter Debow and wife.

1781

Christie, John and Elisabeth—David—April 7.
Wit: David and Wybrech Christie.
Ackerman, Johannis D. and Annatje—David—Sept. 16.
Wit: David and Rachel Hopper.

1785

Vandien, Cornelis (?) and Sierie—Dirk———.
Wit: Jan and Hankee Berdan.

1786

Ackerman, David and Jannetje—David, b. March 26—April 9.
Vande Voor, Paulus and Maria—Daniel, b. June 26—Aug. 13.

1787

Myer, Martin and Gerrebrecht—David, b. March 23—April 15.
Wit: David J. and Margrietje Ackerman.
Messeker, Dirk and Lena—Dirk, b. Oct. 18—Nov. 11.
Spiers, David and Grietje—David—Dec. 30.

1788

EARL, Edward and Abigail—Doosje—May 25.
Wit: Hessel and Catriena Ryerson.
DEFFENDORF, George and Elisabeth—Dolle, b. July 1—Aug. 10.
Wit: Willem and Maragrietje Wannemaker.
DEBAEN, Jacob and Geesje—David, b. Aug. 10—Aug. 31.
HORN, Joseph and Marytje—David, b. Nov. 10—Dec. 21.
Wit: David and Jannetje Ackerman.

1789

DEBAEN, Joost and Grietje—David, b. Jan. 10, 1789————.
Wit: Benjamin and Polle Jero.
MEEBIE, Jan and Lea—David, b. July 15—Aug. 9.
Wit: David and Annaatje Debaen.

1791

HOPPE, Andreas D. and Aaltje—David, b. Sept. 1—Sept. 29.
Wit: David and Rachel Hoppe.

1792

ACKERMAN, David and Metje—David, b. March 17—April 10.
Wit: Gerrit and Elisabeth Ackerman.

1793

LESYIER, Abraham and Annaatje—David, b. Sept. 6, 1792—Feb. 17.
Wit: David and Angenietje Eckerson.
VAN VLERCOM, John and Geertje—David, b. April 24—May 9.
Wit: David and Gerretje Van Vlercom

1794

PERRY, Pieter and Marregrietje - Daniel, b. Jan. 18 - Feb 16.
Wit: Daniel and Jannitje Perry.
VAN WINKEL, Francis and Isabella - David, b. July 13 - Sep. 14.
ECKERSON, Paulus and Maria - David, b. Sep. 12 - Oct. 5.
Wit: David and Angenietje Eckerson.
SYOURT, Adolf and Aaltje - David, b. July 1 - Oct. 5.
Wit: Daniel and Cathalyntje Ackerman.
JERSEY, John and Maria - Daniel, b. Nov. 3 - Nov. 30.
Wit: Daniel and Jannitje Perry.

1795

TAYLOR, Aaron and Jannitje—Dirkje, b. Dec. 4, 1794—Jan. 4.
TAALMAN, Isaack and Cornelia—David, b. Jan. 16—Feb. 8.
Wit: David and Cornelia Bogert.
BERDAN, Johannis and Maria—Dirk, b. April 19—May 14.
HOPPE, Hendrik and Hettie—David, b. Oct. 2—Nov. 1.
Wit: David and Rachel Hoppe.
TERHUNE, Albert and Leah—Dirk, b. Oct. 31—Nov. 22.
Wit: Abraham and Soecke Terhune.
TISE, John and Rachel—David, b. Oct. 26—Dec. 6.

1796

DEBAAN, Abraham and Sara—David, b. Feb. 20—March 6.
Wit: David and Annaatje Debaan.
V[AN] D. VOTE, Paul and Elisabeth—David, b. Feb. 6—March 27.

VANSCHYVEN, Willem and Saartje—Dirk, b. June 25—July 31.
Wit: Dirk and Antje Bos.
VANDIEN, Andries and Saartje—Dirk, b. Aug. 8—Sept. 18.
Wit: Dirk and Maria Vandien.

1797
ECKERSON, Thomas and Susanna—David, b. Jan. 10—Feb. 19.
Wit: David and Angenietje Eckerson.
VAN BLERCOM, John and Geertje—David, b. Feb. 14—March 19.
Wit: David and Gerritje Van Blercom.

1798
Bos, Dirk and Antje—Dirk, b. March 17—April 1.
Wit: Jacob and Selle Vanderbeeck.
HOPPER, Gerrit and Maria—David, b. May 12—July 7.
POTTER, John and Maria—Dolle, b. Nov. 21—Dec. 8.

1800
POULISSON, John and Charitie—David, b. Jan. 3—March 2.
ECKER, Cornelius and Marytje—David, b. Apr. 15—May 11.
BANTA, Abraham and Dievertje—Dievertje, b. Aug. 18—Sept. 14.
QUACKENBUSH, David and Maria—David, b. Sept. 26—Nov. 2.

1756
ALYEE, Hannes and Annatje—Elsie, b. May 11—May 30.
Wit. Cobus and Annatje Alyee.

1758
VANDELINDE, Dom. Benjamin and Elisabeth—Ester, b. Sept. 9—Sept. 18.
Wit: Isack and Janneke Kingsland.
VANBLERKOM, Garrit and Hillegond—Elisabeth—Sept. 24.
Wit: Adriaan and Hendrik Post.
VONCK, Pieter and Marytje—Elisabeth, b. Oct. 17—Nov. 19.
Wit: Joseph and Ariaantje Wessels.

1759
HENNION, David and Willemyntje—Eva, b. Jan. 19—Feb. 18.
Wit: Roelof H. and Annaatje Van Houte.

1761
VAN ZEYL, Pieter and Lena—Egbert, b. Feb. 1.
Wit: Egbert and Saartje Van Zeyl.
ACKERMAN, Hannes I. and Lena—Elisabeth—Aug. 9.
Wit: Willem and Grietje Ackerman.

1764
ACKERMAN, Willem and Grietje—Elisabeth—Feb. 5.
Wit: David J. and Angenietje Ackerman.

1766
DEPUE, Isaac and Brechje—Elisabeth, b. Jan. 4—Feb. 2.
Wit: Petrus and Lisabeth Depue.

1768
SWIN, Pieter and Elisabeth—Elisabeth, b. May 8—June 5.
Wit: Christoffel and Rebecka Sendel.

1769
PERRY, Cobus and Annatje—Elisabeth—Jan. 1.
Wit: Harme and Maria Van Rype.

HOPPE, Andries I. and Elisabeth—Elisabeth—Mar. 26.
Wit: Jan and Elisabeth Hoppe.
VAN BLERKOM, Pieter H. and Jannitje—Elisabeth—Apr. 9.
Wit: Cornelis and Elisabeth Vanhoren.

1770

MESSEKER, Abram and Rachel—Eva—Jan. 14.
Wit: Coenraad and Eva Pielisfelt.

1771

VANBLERCOM, Frans and Jacomyntje—Elisabeth—Feb. 24.
Wit: Cornelis and Elisabeth Vanhoren.
HOPPE, Albert and Rachel—Elisabeth—June 2.
Wit: Johannis and Antje Westervelt.
BOGERT, Jacob and Marytje—Eva—Nov. 10.
Wit: Hendrik Beer.

1772

ACKERMAN, David D. and Lisabeth—Elsje—Feb. 2.
Wit: Abram R. and Jannitje Westervelt

1774

DAVIS, Nikolaas—Egbert—May 8.
Wit: Egbert Van Zeyl.
ZABRISKE, Hendrik C. and Maria—Elisabeth—Aug. 28.
Wit: Christiaan A. and Marytje Zobriskie.
ACKERMAN, Gerrit J. and Rachel—Elisabeth—Sept. 4.
Wit: Cornelis and Elisabeth Ackerman.

1775

BANTA, Thomas W. and Geertruy—Eefje, b. Feb. 13—Apr. 9.

1779

GERRILL, John and Sara—Elisabeth—Apr. 4.

1781

HERS, Hendrik—Elizabeth—July 1.
HENNION, Willem and Eva—Eva, b. June 20—July 1.
Wit: Christiaan and Eva Pulisvelt.

1785

VANDIEN, Andreas and Sara—Elisabeth—Sept. 4.

1786

ACKERMAN, David and Aaltje—Elisabeth, b. May 8—May 14.
Wit: Albert and Elisabeth Terhune.

1787

KNEGT, Coenraad and Grietje—Elisabeth, b. June 11—July 15.
Wit: Hermanus Van Orden; Elisabeth Swin.
VAN BOSKERK, Laurens and Maria—Elisabeth—Dec. 9.
Wit: Johan Jurrie and Elisabeth Snyder.

1788

BERTOLF, Benjamin and Maria—Elisabeth—May 1.
Wit: Jan and Lea Van Imburgh.
HORN, Jacob and Femmetje—Elisabeth, b. July 19—Aug. 10.
Wit: Thomas and Maria Van Boskerk.
BELL, William and Rachel—Elsje Earl—Sept. 8.

1789

SCHUYLER, Adoniah and Elisabeth—Elisabeth—Feb. 17.

ZABRISKE, John and Cornelia—Elisabeth, b. Feb. 13—Mar. 1.
Wit: Thomas and Maria Vandien.

WILSON, Albert and Maria—Elisabeth, b. June 6—June 15.

MYER, Marten and Brechje—Elisabeth, b. Sept. 5—Oct. 11.

1790

VANDERBEEK, Arie and Lena—Elisabeth, b. Jan. 8—Jan. 31.
Wit: Thomas and Angenietje Toers.

EARLE, Edward and Abigael—Enoch—Aug. 15.
Wit: Jacobus G. and Rachel Ackerman.

ACKERMAN, David and Aaltje—Elisabeth, b. Aug. 24—Sept. 13.
Wit: Albert and Elisabeth Terhune.

1791

GOETSCHIUS, Samuel and Elisabeth—Elisabeth, b. Dec. 29, 1790—Jan. 30.

JURRIE, John and Elisabeth—Elisabeth—Feb. 6.

DIETER, Adam and Rosina—Elisabeth, b. Sept. 14—Oct. 2.
Wit: Casparus Berberie; Polla Goetschius.

FISHER, Coenraad and Maria—Elisabeth, b. Aug. 18—Oct. 2.
Wit: Hendrik and Maritje Bos.

1792

SHARP, Morris and Elisabeth—Elisabeth, b. Sept. 15—Nov. 11.
Wit: James Stagge; Ariaantje Myer.

1793

BOGERT, Steven and Maria—Effie, b. Feb. 22—Mar. 24.

BANTA, Samuel and Elisabeth—Elisabeth, b. May 12—June 9.
Wit: David Beyerd; Betsey Bayard.

BOURGEES, Daniel and Maragrietje—Elisabeth, b. Sept. 3—Sept. 22.

SMITH, Pieter and Grietje—Elisabeth, b. Aug. 11—Oct. 20.

1794

WILSON, Albert and Maria—Eliah, b. Dec. 16, 1793—Jan. 26.

GOETSCHIUS, John and Annatje—Elisabeth, b. Jan. 18—Mar. 16.

COLE, Adriaan and Elisabeth—Elisabeth, b. Sept. 7—Oct. 26.

YOUMANS, Daniel and Catrina—Elisabeth, b. Oct. 25—Nov. 16.

DURIE, Jan and Annatje—Elisabeth, b. Oct. 17—Dec. 7.
Wit: Johannes and Saartje Ackerman.

1795

POLHEMIUS, Theodorus and Elisabeth—Elisabeth, b. Aug. 3—Aug. 23.

SWIN, Hendrik and Rachel—Elisabeth, b. Nov. 22—Dec. 25.

1796

RYERS, Jan and Maria—Elisabeth, b. Jan. 17—Jan. 31.

1797

VAN HOORN, Cornelis and Jannetje—Elisabeth, b. Jan. 8—Feb. 19.

EARL, Edward and Abigail—Elisabeth, b. Sept. 22—Oct. 8.

VANORDEN, John and Tryntje—Elisabeth, b. Nov. 9—Dec. 24.

1798

SISCO, Willem and Elsiabeth—Elisabeth, b. Feb. 12—Apr. 1.

1799

ECKERSON, Edward and Hatty—Elisabeth, b. Oct. 26, 1798—Jan. 6.
WORTENDYK, Jacob and Elisabeth—Elisabeth, b. June 20—July 7.
HOPPER, Nicasie and Maria—Elisabeth, b. May 28—July 7.
VAN AULEN, Gerrit and Geertje—Effie, b. June 1—July 7.

1800

ZABRISKIE, John and Margarit—Elisabeth, b. Dec. 19, 1799—Jan. 23.
HEMMION, Nicholaas and Leentje—Elisabeth, b. Jan. 13—Jan. 26.
DERYEA, Samuel and Catriena—Elisabeth, b. Feb. 18—Mar. 12.
STUDS, Henry and Margaret—Elisabeth, b. May 4—July 20.
BARR, David and Mary—Elisabeth, b. April 13—Sept. 21.

1751

RYERSE, Hannes W. and Marytje—Frans—Mar. 17.
Wit: Teunis and Lena Ryerse.

1765

NIX, Christoffel and Sara—Femmitje, b. Mar. 22—May 5.
Wit: Egbert and Saartje V. Zeyl.

1768

VAN RYPE, Harme and Maria—Frederik—Aug. 28.
Wit: Frederik and Antje Van Rype.

1773

VAN BLERKOM, David J. and Gerritje—Fytje—June 27.
Wit: Isaac and Fytje Meaby.
SWAN, Rachel—Frances—July 11.
Wit: Gerrit J. and Elsje Hoppe.

1775

WESTERVELT, Pieter and Cathalyntje—Fytje, b. Dec. 5, 1774—Jan. 2.

1776

MYER, Jacob D. and Ellie—Fytje—Apr. 7.
ODEL, Gerrit and Rebecka—Frances—Feb. 16.
Wit: Keetje Hoogland.

1787

DEMAREST, Samuel and Catriena—Francyntje, b. Jan. 13—Feb. 11.
Wit: Barend and Francyntje Fersyeur.
BLAUVELT, Cornelis and Catriena—Francyntje, b. Aug. 5—Aug. 26.
Wit: Barend and Francyntje Fersyeur.

1794

TAYLOR, Aaron and Jannetje—Phebe, b. Oct. 23, 1792—Mar. 16.
JUREY, John and Elisabeth—Fredrikus, b. Nov. 15—Dec. 14.
Wit: William and Susanna Jurey.

1795

CROUT, John and Phebe—Phebe, b. Feb. 7—Apr. 12.

1796

DEBAAN, Andreas and Jannitje—Francyntje, b. Dec. 17, 1795—Jan. 1.
Wit: Barend and Francyntje Fersyeur.

1798

WOERTENDYK, John and Elisabeth—Fredrik, b. Feb. 6—Feb. 11.
Wit: Neesje Poost.

1750
ZABRISKIE, Jacob C. and Lena—Gerrit—Sept. 23.
Wit: Albert and Rachel Ackerman.
ZABRISKIE, Hendrik C. and Neesje—Geertje—Nov. 11.
Wit: Hartman and Lea Cadmus.

1752
HARMANUS, Nix[1]—Geertje—Aug. 2.
Wit: Cornelius C. Dugrau.

1753
SYOURT, Willem and Trintje—Grietje—Dec. 2.
Wit: Christiaan and Grietje Wannemaker.

1754
ODEL, Benjamin and Nellie—Gerrit—July 28.
Wit: Gerrit I. and Elsje Hoppe.
WESTERVELT, Cornelius J. and Jannike—Gerrit, b. July 19—Aug. 4.
Wit: Hendrik and Lisabeth Lutkins.

1755
BONGAERT, Lucas and Doritie—Geertje—Aug. 3.
Wit: Albert H. and Jannitje Terhuyn.
DUGRAU, Abel and Maaike—Geertje—Sept. 14.
Wit: Barend and Rachel Vanhoren.
LUTKINS, Hendrik and Lisabeth—Gerrit—Sept. 14.
Wit: Cornelius I. and Janneke Westervelt.

---

[1]Probably Nix, Harmanus.—EDITOR.

1756

ACKERMAN, Gerrit and Lena—Gerrit—Feb. 1.
Wit: Adam and Rachel Van Voorhees.
ZABRISKE, Jacob H. and Wyntje—Geertrui—Oct. 17.
Wit: Abram and Marytje Terhuyn.
ACKERMAN, David D. and Annatje—Grietje—Dec. 25.
Wit: Harmanus and Aaltje Vanblerkom.

1757

ALYEE, Isaac and Annaatje—Margrietje, b. Jan. 6—Jan. 16.
Wit: Pieter and Margrietje Alyee.
HOPPE, Albert and Rachel—Gerrit—Feb. 6.
Wit: Gerrit and Elsie Hoppe.
HOPPE, Abram and Rebecka—Gerrit, b. Jan. 29—Mar. 12.
Wit: Jan and Jannitje Dykman.

1758

TERHUYN, Abram and Marytje—Geertrui—Feb. 26.
Wit: Jacob H. and Wyntje Zabriskie.

1759

HOPPE, Willem and Antje—Gerrit—Sept. 30.
Wit: Gerrit A. and Hendrikje Hoppe.

1761

TERHUYN, Abraham and Marytje—Geertje, b. June 5.
Wit: Jacob H. and Wyntje Zabriskie.

1764

HELM, Samuel and Trientje—Geertje, b. Oct. 26—Nov. 25.
Wit: Cornelis and Arianntje Myer.

1765

ACKERMAN, Albert and Rachel—Gerrit—Dec. 15.
Wit: Albert C. and Aaltje Zabriske.

1766

VANHOREN, Lucas and Grietje—Gerrit, b. Apr. 9—May 1.
Wit: Gerrit and Jacomyntje Dumaree.

1767

HOPPE, Jan J. and Geertje—Gerrit—Sept. 27.
Wit: Gerrit and Elsje Hoppe.
HOPPE, Gerrit A. and Margrietje—Gerrit, b. Nov. 11—Dec. 6.
Wit: Hendrik and Wyntje Hoppe.

1768

DUMAREE, Pieter P. and Lydea—Gerrit—June 19.
Wit: Andries G. and Abigail Hoppe.
ZABRISKE, Albert J. and Geesje—Gerrit—Sept. 4.
VANBLERKOM, David and Elisabeth—Gerrit—Sept. 25.
Wit: Cobus and Antje Parrelman.

1769

ACKERMAN, Abram and Marietje—Gerrit—June 25.
Wit: Albert and Rachel Ackerman.

1770

HOPPE, Pieter and Annetje—Gerrit—Feb. 19.
Wit: Gerrit H. and Antje Hoppe.
KIP, Isaac N. and Hendrikje—Grietje, b. Mar. 10—Apr. 8.
Wit: Nicasie and Grietje Kip.
DUMAREE, Pieter P. and Lydea—Gerrit, b. Nov. 28—Dec. 25.
Wit: Gerrit A. and Rachel Hoppe.

1772

VANDIEN, Thomas and Polly—Gerrit—Feb. 16.
Wit: Andries and Sarah Vandien.
PILESFELT, Willem and Lisabeth—Geertje—Nov. 8.
Wit: Jacob and Ebbi Myer.

1773

ACKERMAN, Albert G. and Antje—Grietje—Mar. 7.
Wit: Jacob and Grietje Stor.
HOPPE, Jan. J. A. and Jannitje—Geertje, b. Apr. 1—May 2.
Wit: Jan. Hoppe, Jr., and Alltje Hoppe.
HOPPE, Pieter and Annitje—Geesje—May 2.
Wit: Hessel and Geesje Doremus.
BANTA, Thomas—Geesje—Sept. 26.
Wit: Geertje Banta.

1774

ACKERMAN, Willem and Grietje—Gerrit—Feb. 6.
Wit: Gerrit J. and Rachel Ackerman.
DUMAREE, Samuel B. and Rebecka—Geesje—May 29.
Wit: Jacobus and Geesje Deryee.
HOPPE, Jan. J. and Aaltje—Geertje—Aug. 7.
Wit: Jan Clase and Marytje Zabriskie.
RIDDENAAR, Coenraad and Lisabeth—Grietje, b. July 29—Aug. 7.
Wit: Hans and Antje Ridnaar.
ACKERMAN, David G. and Aaltje—Gerrit—Sept. 4.
Wit: Johannes and Lena Ackerman.
HOPPE, Andries G. and Trientje—Gerrit—Sept. 18.
Wit: Gerrit A. and Rachel Hoppe.
ACKERMAN, David D. and Lisabeth—Gerrit—Sept. 25.
Wit: Gerrit D. and Lena Ackerman.

1775

DUBOW, Pieter A. and Brechje—Gerrit—Apr. 2.
Wit: Jacobus and Antje Parrelman.
HOPPE, Andries I. and Lisabeth—Geertje—Sept. 17.
Wit: Benjamin and Annatje Zabriske.

1776

WESTERVELT, Casparus and Rachel—Geertje, b. Feb. 12—Mar. 10.
STEKER, Nathes and Lisabeth—Grietje—Mar. 17.
Wit: Jacob Valentyne; Grietje Valentyne.
BREVOORT, Samuel and Martynyje—Grietje—Apr. 21.
Wit: Johannis and Grietje Brevoort.
ALLEN, John and Margaret—Guy—Oct. 14.

1780

PERKHOFF, Hendrik and Polly—Geesje—Mar. 19.
Wit: Cornelis and Geesje Vanhoren.
VANBLERCOM, Samuel and Sucke—Gerrit—Nov. 19.

1782

VANHORN, Daniel and Antje—Grietje—Feb. 25.
HERRING, Cornelis—Gerrit, b Dec. 9, 1781—Jan. 6.
Wit: Gerrit Ariaanse.

1783

HALDRUM, Nicolaas and Marretje—Geertje.
Wit: Abraham Haldrum and wife Judik.

1782

BOGERT, Steven—Geesje—Dec. 4.
HOPPE, Steven and Giertje—Gerrit—July 25.
Wit: Andries and Tryntje Hoppe.

1783

LOURENS—Grietje—Apr. 26.

1784

ECKERSE, Edward—Grietje—Apr. 25.
BEL, Bellie and Rachel—Gerrit Jan Hoppe, b. Apr. 1—May 16.
Wit: Jan Hoppe and wife.
HOPPE. Jan J. and Catharina— Geertje—Apr. 10.
Wit: Albert Van Voorhees and wife.

1785

HOPPE, Hendrik and Rachel—Gerrit, b. June 11—July 3.
Wit. Gerrit and Antje Hoppe.
MOLGRAF, Boljer and Christien—Grietje—Sep. 4.
Wit: Lodewyk and Grietje Fisher
ZABRISKE, Abraham and Maria—Gerrit—Sept. 11.
Wit: Gerrit Zabriske.
BELL, Wm. M. and Rachel—Gerard De Peyster—Sep. 25.
Wit: Gerard De Peyster and Sally Swartwout.
VANDIEN, Albert and Polly—Gerrit—Nov. 13.
Wit: Cornelis and Sara Vandien.

1786

DE BAAN, Jan and Wyntje—Gerrit, b. Jan. 11—Feb. 5.
Wit: Gerrit and Cathalyntje Durie.
SMYTH, Albert and Susanna—Gerrit, b. Mar. 11—Apr. 9.
Wit: Gerrit and Hester Smith.
HOPPE, Gerrit and Maria—Gerrit, b. June 24—July 9.
Wit: Arie and Christina Ackerman.
QUIN, Tertullian and Elsje—Grietje, b. July 4—Sep. 10.
VAN BLERKOM, Petrus and Jannetje—Gerrit, b. Oct. 10—Oct. 22.
Wit: Gerrit and Rachel Ackerman.
Bos, Dirk and Antje—Grietje, b. Nov. 13—Dec. 24.
Wit: Pieter and Grietje Bos.

1787

BERTOLF, Jacobus and Lea—Guliaam, b. Dec. 22, 1786—Jan. 28.
GOETSCHIUS, Piatus and Catriena—Grietje, b. Dec. 28, 1786—Jan. 28.
VAN RYPE, Herman and Maria—Gerrit, b. Mar. 29—May 6.
  Wit: Gerrit and Abigail Van Rype.
DEBAAN, Petrus and Maria—Grietje—Sep. 16.
POST, Pieter I. and Rachel—Grietje, b. Nov. 27—Dec. 25.
  Wit: Pieter and Nellie Davis.

1788

VANDIEN, Harmen and Aaltje—Gerrit—May 1.
  Wit: Albert and Maria Vandien.
ZABRISKIE, Hendrik and Maria—Gerrit—June 22.
POST, Jacob and Sara—Gerrit, b. Aug. 5—Aug. 31.
BOS, Lodewyk and Leentje—Grietje, b. Nov. 22—Dec. 21.
  Wit: Hendrik and Maria Bos.
SERVENT, John and Grietje—Grietje, b. Nov. 20—Dec. 21.

1789

BOS, Pieter and Frone—Grietje, b. Feb. 15—Mar. 1.
  Wit: Pieter and Grietje Watkins.
HOPPE, Jan J. and Catriena—Gerrit and Jan (twins), b. Feb. 7—Mar. 1.

1791

ACKERMAN, Jacobus G. and Rachel—Gerardus, b. Mar. 20—Apr. 3.
  Wit: Gerrit G. Ackerman and wife.

1792

HOPPE, Hendrik and Aaltje-Geertje, b. Mar 10-Apr 10.
  Wit: Abraham J. and Geeertje Hoppe.
BANTA, Johannis and Tryntje—Gerrit, b. Mar. 10—Apr. 10.
  Wit: Gerrit and Cathalyntje Durie.

1794

OLDIS, Gerrit and Rebecka—Gerrit, b. May 25—June 22.
  Wit: Jan and Rachel Hoppe.
HOPPE, John and Maria—Gerrit, b. July 2—July 27.
  Wit: Gerrit and Maria Hoppe.

1795

ZABRISKE, Jacob and Elisabeth—Geesje, b. Feb. 8—Feb. 19.
  Wit: Gerrit and Maria Zabriske.
CROUTER, John and Maragrietje—George, b. Mar. 11—Apr. 12.

1796

POST, Pieter and Neesje—Gerrit, b. Dec. 16, 1795—Feb. 28.
WREYGHT, Albert and Annaatje—Geertje, b. Aug. 7—Sep. 18.
HOPPE, Abraham and Geertje—Geertje, b. Nov. 3—Dec. 25.

1797

VANDIEN, Cornelis and Margrietje—Gerrit, b. Apr. 8—Apr. 23.

1798

HOPPE, Jan G. (?) and Rachel—Gerrit, b. Apr. 7—May 29.
FLEISCHMAN, Abraham and Sophia Elisabeth—George Scriba, b. July
  29—Sep. 9.

BLAUVELT, Abraham and Elisabeth—Geertje, b. July 24—Aug. 11.
Wit: Isaac and Geertje Blauvelt.

1799
HOPPER, Albert and Elisabeth—Gerrit, b. Oct. 20—Nov. 10.
ACKERMAN, John and Maria—Gerrit, b. Apr. 24—June 2.

1800
SMITH, Gerrit and Hetty—Gerrit, b. Nov. 30—Dec. 7.

1749
STEVENS, Nathaniel and Lea—Hendrik—May 21.
Wit: Hendrik and Grietje Riddenaar.
WANNEMAKER, Pieter and Marytje—Hendrik—Nov. 26.
Wit: Joost and Elisabeth Schyourt.
RUTAN, Hannes and Aaltje—Hannes—Nov. 26.
Wit: Dennis D. and Lea Rutan.

1751
VANDERBEEK, Paulus and Rachel—Hannes—June 14.
Wit: Hannes and Marytje Van Blercom.

1752
ZABRISKIE, Jacob H. and Wyntje—Hendrikus—Mar. 8.
Wit: Hendrik and Geertje Zabriskie.
Vos, Hendrik and Anna Margrit—Hendrik—Aug. 9.
Wit: Coenraad and Marytje Wannemaker.
Vos, Philip and Lisabeth—Hendrik and Coenradus (twins)—Aug. 9.
Wit: Hendrik and Anna Margriet Vos; Coenraad and Catriena
Muyseger.
STORM, Hendrik and Cornelia—Hendrik—Oct. 16.
Wit: Jurrien and Marytje Vanderbeek.

1754
DUREMES, Hessel and Geesje—Hendrik—Apr. 28.
Wit: Hendrik and Lybe Van Ale.
TERHUYN, Dirk and Lea—Hendrikus—May 4.
Wit: Hendrik and Geertje Zobrowiske.
VAN ZEYL, Pieter and Lena—Hannes—May 4.
Wit: Hans and Lena Van Zeyl.

1756
ACKERMAN, Pieter and Antje—Hendrik—Feb. 5.
Wit: Steven and Tryntje Zoberewiske.
WANNEMAKER, Harmanus and Susanna—Hendrik, b. Dec. 23, 1755—
Mar. 7.
Wit: Hendrik and Lisabeth Wannemaker.
SLINGERLAND, Teunis—Hendrik and Abram (twins)—May 9.
Wit: Abel and Maaike Degrau; Joshua S. and Lisabeth Bos.
VAN ZEYL, Pieter and Lena—Hermanus—May 9.
Wit: Hermanus Vanblerkom.
(Name of second witness obliterated).

1757
LAROY, Cobus and Rebecka—Hendrik—Dec. 4.
Wit: Lambert and Lybe Laroy.

1758
LUTKENS, Hendrik and Leybe—Harme—Feb. 12.
Wit: Hannes and Maritje Vanhoren.

1759
HOPPE, Andries and Marytje—Hendrik—Sep. 9.
Wit: Hendrik and Wyntje Hoppe.

1760
HOPPE, Hendrik A. and Wyntje—Hendrik—Feb. 17.
Wit: Jan. A. and Lisabeth Hoppe.
DEGRAU, Klaes and N. N.—Hermanus—Mar. 23.
Wit: Lucas and N. N. Van Blerkum.

1761
BOGERT, Jacob and Marytje—Hendrik—May 24.
Wit: Hendrik and Antje Beer.

1762
BANTA, Jacob and Lena—Hendrik—Sep. 12.
Wit: Hendrik and Sara Banta.

1763
TERHUYN, Abram and Marytje—Hendrikus or Hendrika—Aug. 7.
Wit: Albert H. and Telletje Zabriske.
VAN ZEYL, Hannes A. and Catriena—Hendrik—Aug. 7.
Wit: Hendrik and Marytje Messeker.

1764
TRAPHAGE, Hendrik and Claartje—Hendrik—June 10.
Wit: Gerrit H. and Antje Hoppe.

1765
DERYIE, Daniel and Vrouwtje—Hendrika—Feb. 10.
Wit: Jan R. and Hendrika Berdan.
ALYEE, Abram—Hendrik—Oct. 13.
LUTKENS, Harme and Antje—Hendrik—Nov. 24.
Wit: Hendrik and Lybe Lutkens.

1767
V. DIEN, Gerrit and Sara—Harme—Jan. 25.
Wit: Harme and Antje Lutkins.
BOGERT, Jacob and Marytje—Jannitje—Apr. 24.
Wit: Jacob J. and Jannitje Zobriske.
HOPPE, Abram H. and Antje—Hendrik—July 5.
Wit: Hendrik and Wyntje Hoppe.
HOPPE, David and Rachel—Hendrik—Aug. 30.
Wit: Abram H. and Antje Hoppe.

1768
RITE, Willem and Aaltje—Hendrik—Sep. 19.
Wit: Hendrik Ackerman and Lea A. Zabriske.

1769
BROUWER, Abram D.—Hans—June 4.
Wit: Brechje Van Blercom.
RIDNAER, Hendrik H. and Marytje—Hendrik—July 23.
Wit: Hendrik and Margrit Ridnaer.
TERHUYN, Samuel and Lea—Hendrik—Dec. 3.
Wit: Hendrik C. and Maria Zabriske.
VAN IMBURGH, John and Antje—Hendrik—Dec. 31.
Wit: Hannes and Ariaantje Van Imburgh.

1770
RIDDENAAR, Hannes and Nansje—Hendrik, b. May 5—May 20.
Wit: Hendrik H. and Marytje Riddenaar.

CLERCK, Jacobus D. and Neeltje—Hermanus, b. Apr. 11—May 27.
Wit: Harmanus and Rebecca Taelman.
HOPPE, Abram H. and Antje—Hendrik—June 4.
Wit: Hendrik and Aaltje H. Hoppe.
TRAPHAGE, Hendrik—Hannes—June 4.
Wit: Paulus J. and Rachel Vanderbeek.
V. HOUTEN, Adriaan and Maritje—Helmeg—June 4.
Wit: Abram and Lea Cadmus.

1771
LUTKINS, Jan and Grietje—Harme—June 30.
Wit: Hendrik and Lybe Lutkins.
HOPPE, Andries J. and Lisabeth—Hester—June 30.
Wit: Abram J. and Brechje Ackerman.
SWIN, Pieter and Lisabeth—Hendrik, b. Aug. 14—Sep. 15.
Wit: Hendrik and Crastina Ryke.

1772
HOPPE, Jan H. and Fytje—Hessel—Mar. 15.
Wit: Pieter H. and Antje Hoppe.
VAN RYPE, Gerret and Abigael—Hendrika—Apr. 15.
Wit: Gerrit A. and Rachel Hoppe.
HOPPE, Andries G. and Lea—Hendrika—June 9.
Wit: Gerrit A. and Rachel Hoppe.

1774
LUTKENS, Harme and Antie—Harme—Feb. 26.
Wit: Pieter and Annatje Lutkens.
VAN GELDER, Jonathan and Rachel—Hittie, b. Oct. 23—Nov. 20.

1775
JENKENS, Lambertus and Annatje—Hannes, b. Jan. 24—Feb. 19.
Wit: Cobus H. and Trientje Bertolf.
VALENTYNE, Jacob and Grietje—Hantice—Feb. 19.
Wit: Mathys Valentine.
BOGERT, Jacob and Marytje—Hendrik—May 28.
Wit: Jacob Ja. and Aaltje Zobriske.
VAN BLERKOM, Pieter H. and Jannitje—Harmanus—June 9.
Wit: Hannes J. and Lena Ackerman.

1779
HOPPE, Andries G. and Tryntje—Hendrik—Dec. 12.
Wit: Gerrit H. and Antje Hoppe.

1782
STOERM, Staats—Hendrik—Jan. 11.
Wit: Hendrik.

1784
HOPPE, Pieter—Hendrik—May 16.
Wit: Hendrik Dremes and wife.
TERHUNE, Jan—Harmen—July 11.
Wit: Harmen Lutkins and wife.
STORM, Staats ————————

1794

WESTERVELT, Albert and Margrietje—Hendrik, b. May 19—June 22.

MESSEKER, Helmegh and Fytje—Hendrik, b. May 24—June 22.

VANHOORN, Pieter and Rachel Van Gelder—Hettie, b. Mar. 15—June 22.

1795

TERHUEN, Hendrik and Rachel—Hendrikje, b. Mar. 27—Apr. 19.
Wit: Gerrit and Abigail Van Rype.

MESSEKER, Lodewyk and Sara—Hendrik—Oct. 18.
Wit: Edward and Abigail Earle.

BOSCH, Samuel and Lena—Hendrik, b. Sep. 22—Dec. 25.

1796

ROTAN, Abraham and Maria—Hendrik, b. Oct. 25—Dec. 25.
Wit: Hendrik and Jannitje Terhuen.

1797

BOS, Reinhart and Elisabeth—Hendrik, b. May 21—June 4.
Wit: Isaak and Maria Vrerikse.

ZABRISKA, Cornelius and Maria—Hendrik, b. Nov. 5—Nov. 26.
Wit: Hendrik and Maria Zabriske.

ACKERMAN, Abraham and Salome—Hendrik, b. Nov. 28—Dec. 24.

1798

ZABRISKE, Jan J. and Margrietje—Hendrikje, b. Dec. 23, 1797—Feb. 5.
Wit: Gerrit and Abigail Van Rype.

LUTKENS, Stephen and Rachel—Harmen, b. Feb. 13—Mar. 4.

CHRISTOPHER, John and Aaltje—Hendrik, b. Feb. 23—Mar. 4.

1800

VAN RYPEN, Frederik and Maria—Harmen, b. May 24—June 29.
Wit: Harmen and Maria Van Rypen.

1785

BOGERT, Jacob—Hendrik—Apr. 10.
Wit: Jacob Bogert and wife Maria.

ZABRISKIE, Hendrik I. and Polly—Hendrikus—Aug. 14.
Wit: Wyntje I. Zabriske.

1786

VERVELEN, Gideon and Maria—Hendrik, b. Dec. 1, 1785—Jan. 29.
Wit: Cornelis and Catrina Eckerson.

1787

SLOT, Isaac and Lea—Helena, b. July 28—Aug. 26.
Wit: Christiaan J. and Maria Zabriskie.

TRAPHAGE, Jonathan H. and Polly—Hendrik—Sep. 16.
Wit: Hendrik and Grietje Traphage.

1788

TRAPHAGE, Jonathan and Catriena—Hendrik—Jan. 1.
Wit: Hendrik and Grietje Traphage.

JERSEY, Pieter and Annaatje—Hendrik, b. Mar. 4—Apr. 20.
Wit: Jan and Grietje Servent.

VAN BLERCOM, David and Maria—Harman—June 22.

GERRITSEN, Johannis and Maria—Hessel, b. July 11—July 27.
Wit: Abraham and Catriena Cadmus.

GERRITSON, Johannis H. and Maria—Hessel, b. July 13—Aug.
Wit: Hessel and Sara Gerritson.

1789

Bos, Dirk and Antje—Hendrik—Apr. 29.

ZABRISKE, Jan J. and Hendrikje—Hendrikje, b. Apr. 20—June 7.
Wit: Gerrit and Abigail Van Rype.

ZABRISKE, Abraham and Maria—Hendrik, b. July 28—Aug. 9.

1790

SHARP, Morris and Elisabeth—Hester—Dec. 12.

1791

SMITH, Gerrit and Hette—Hette, b. Jan. 4—Jan. 30.
Wit: Hendrik and Hette Frerikse.

PULESVELT, Petrus and Nense—Hendrik, b. June 25—July 24.
Wit: Hendrik and Cornelia Pulesvelt.

DATIE, John and Polly—Hannah, b. Aug. 1—Aug. 21.
Wit: Abraham and Hannah Datie.

1792

BOUMAN, Michael and Maria—Hermanus—Feb. 26.
Wit: Hermanus and Maria Kerlogh.

POULUSSE, John and Klaasje—Hendrik, b. Jan. 7—Feb. 26.
Wit: Hendrik and Jacomyntje Hoppe.

GOETSCHIUS, Piatus and Catriena—Hester—Apr. 10.

HOPPE, Gerrit J. and Maria—Hendrik, b. Aug. 20—Sep. 16.
Wit: Hendrik and Jannetje Terhuen.

ECKERSON, Nikolaes and Maria—Hendrik, b. Oct. 18—Nov. 11.
Wit: Hendrik and Maria Oldis.

1793

SICKELSEN, Jacobus and Maria—Henricus—Mar. 10.

1770

BANTA, Wiert C. and Elisabeth—Jan—July 29.
Wit: Jan C. Banta; Annatje Banta.

MACDANEL, Cornelis—Jan, b. Sept. 4—Oct. 8.

VAN HOUTE, Isaac and Maria—Jacobus—Nov. 4.
Wit: Jacobus and Mettie Post.

————and————Junici—Dec. 2.
Wit: Cobus and Jannitje V. Voorhese.

V. BLERKOM, David and Lisabeth—Jacobus—Dec. 25.
Wit: Albert and Gerrebrecht V. Blerkom.

1771

ALYEE, Isaac and Annaatje—Jacob, b. Jan. 17—Feb. 3.
Wit: Jacob T. and Jannitje Eckerson.

RITE, Willem and Aaltje—Jan—Feb. 24.
Wit: Jan and Styntje Ackerman.

VANORDER, Jan and Jannitje—Jan—Feb. 24.
Wit: Abram J. and Santje Vanderbeek.

TERHUYN, Abram and Marytje—Jacob—Mar. 17.
Wit: Hendrik J. and Marytje Zabriskie.

BLAUVELT, Cobus and Jannitje—Johannes, b. Mar. 2—Apr. 1.
Wit: Johannis and Rachel Blauvelt.

ACKERMAN, Gerrit and Rachel—Jacobus—June 9.
Wit: Jacobus and Jannitje V. Voorhese.

DUMAREE, Benjamin and Lidea—Jannitje—June 23.
Wit: Pieter B. and Jannitje Dumaree.

PEEK, David and Sarah—Jacobus, b. June 18—July 21.
Wit: Jacobus and Willempje Peek.

KOM, Johannis V[an] B[lar] and Rebecka—Johannis, b. July 9—July 21.
Wit: Johannis and Marytje V[an] B[lar] Kom.

MOURUSSE, Jacobus and Lena—Isaac, b. July 24—Aug. 11.
Wit: Isaac and Marytje Mourusse.

ZABRISKIE, Jacob J. and Aaltje—Jacob—Sept. 1.
Wit: Dirk and Lea Terhuyn.

ACKERMAN, Cornelis and Lisabeth—Johannis—Sept. 15.
Wit: Petrus and Maria Ackerman.

VANBOSKERCK, Jan J. and Hester—Johannis, b. May 30—Oct. 2.
Wit: Hannes and Grietje Brevoort.

PIETERSE, Niklaas and Maria—Jan—Nov. 3.
Wit: Willem Pieterse.

ACKERMAN, Hannes J. and Lena—Jannitje—Dec. 1.
Wit: Cobus and Jannitje V. Voorhese.

RYKE, Hendrik and Crestina—Jannitje—Dec. 26.
Wit: David P. Dumaree.

ECKERSON, Phlip—Jacob—Dec. 29.

1772

GARDINIER, Jan and Jacomyntje—Jacob—Feb. 16.
Wit: Jacob and Rachel Banta.

ZABRISKIE, Hendrik J. and Willempje—Jacob—July 5.
Wit: Jacob H. and Wyntje Zabriskie.

HOPPE, Abram and Antje—Jacob—Aug. 16.
Wit: Johannes A. Terhuyn; Marytje Zabriskie.

HOPPE, Gerrit J. and Marytje—Jan—Aug. 16.
Wit: Jan and Elisabeth Hoppe.

BANTA, Cornelis A. and Maria—Joseph, b. Aug. 15—Sept. 27.
Wit: Isaac and Annatje Alyee.

COCKROW, Niklaas and Pietertje—Josie—Nov. 8.
Wit: Pieter and Lena Van Zeyl.

ZABRISKE, Albert J. and Geesje—Jacob—Dec. 6.
Wit: Jacob J. and Jannitje Zabriske.

ACKERMAN, Arie and Maria—Johannis, b. Dec. 3—Dec. 6.
Wit: Hannes A. and Jacomyntje Ackerman.

1773

ACKERMAN, David A. and Jacomyntje—Isaac—Jan. 3.
Wit: Isaac and Saartje Storm.

OOLDES, Hendrik and Marytje—Johannes—May 30.
Wit: Jan J. and Aaltje Hoppe.

ZABRISKIE, Jacob H. and Wyntje—Jannitje—June 27.
Wit: David and Jannitje Dumaree.

VAN ORDER, Jan P. and Jannitje—Jannitje—Aug. 22.
Wit: Willem Smith; Jannitje V. Blerkom.

MILTENBERRI, Luwis and Lisabeth—Joannes—Nov. 7.
Wit: Petrus and Antje Van Blerkom.

PERRI, Daniel and Jannitje—Isaac—Dec. 18.
Wit: Isaac and Grietje Perri.

1774

MESSEKER, Abram and Rachel—Johannis—Jan. 16.
Wit: David D. and Lisabeth Ackerman.

VAN WINKEL, Paulus and Emitje—Jacob—Jan. 23.
Wit: Jacob J. and Jannitje Zabriskie.

STORM, Isaac and Saartje—Jacob—Jan. 23.
Wit: Jacob and Jannitje Storm.

TRAPHAGE, Hendrik and Claartje—John—Mar. 20.
Wit: Jan J. and Aaltje Hoppe.

TRAPHAGE, Jonathan and Catriena—Jacobus, b. Feb. 7—Mar. 27.
Wit: Jacobus and Jannitje Van Gelder.

ZABRISKIE, Christiaan J. and Maria—Jacob—Apr. 24.
Wit: Jacob C. Zabriske.

JERSEY, Peter and Annatje—Jannitje, b. May 6—May 29.
Wit: Abram J. and Ginne Post.

MOURUSSE, Mourus and Tryntje—Jacob, b. Mar. 26—June 28.
Wit: Jacob and Trnytje Mourusse.

VANDERHOEF, Dirk and Catriena—Jacob, b. Feb. 13—June 28.

MICKLER, Hannes and Margrietje—Margrietje and Johannis—Aug. 21.
Wit: For Johannis, Hannes and Rebecca Van Blerkom.

TOIRS, Niklaas and Lisabeth—Jacob, b. Sep. 19—Oct. 30.
Wit: Jacob and Saartje Hoppe.

1775

VAN BLERKOM, Isaac and Sara—Isaac—Jan. 29.
Wit: Hannes and Rebecka Van Blerkom.

DEGROOT, Jacobus—Jacobus—Feb. 2.
Wit: Johannis and Marytje Moore.

ACKERMAN, David A. and Jacomyntje—Jacob—Feb. 19.
Wit: Jan. and Marytje Eckerson.

HOPPE, Albert and Rachel—Jacob—Mar. 12.
Wit: John and Antje Vanimburgh.

ZABRISKE, Abram A. and Maria—John—Apr. 2.
Wit: Jan A. Terhuyn and Geertje J. Zabriskie.

DUBAEN, Joost and Grietje—Jacob, b. Mar. 21—Apr. 9.
Wit: Jacob and Marytje Dubaen.

MABIE, Jan and Lea—Jannitje, b. July 2—Apr. 9.
Wit: Pieter and Jannitje Mabie.

MYER, Hannes C. and Sara—Jannitje, b. June 27—July 9.
Wit: Isaac and Jannitje Post.

TERHUYN, Steven and Jannitje—Jan—Aug. 27.
Wit: Jan D. and Marytje Terhuyn.

HOPPE, Andries A. and Lisabeth—Jannitje—Nov. 15.
Wit: Abram H. and Antje Hoppe.

1776

HERMERSTOND, James—James—Jan. 7.

POST, Isaac and Jannitje—Jannitje—Mar. 10.

JURRY, Fredrik and Marter—Jones, b. Dec. 9, 1775—Mar. 31.

PERRY, Daniel and Jannitje—Jannitje, b. Mar. 15—Apr. 7.
Wit: Cobus and Annaatje Perry.

HOPPE, Gerrit J. and Marytje—Jacob—Apr. 14.
Wit: Jacob H. and Wyntje Zabriske.

DAVIS, Niklaas and Maria—Johannis—May 6.
Wit: Pieter and Lena Van Zeyl.

BROWER, Widow Antje—Jacobus—June 16.
Wit: Abram J. and Santje Vanderbeek.

DAVIS, Niklaas—Johannis—July 24.
Wit: Hermanus and Saaartje Van Zeyl.

———, ——— and ——— —Johannis—July 24.
Wit: Harme and Antje Lutkens.

1780

BOGERT, Cobus J. and Cornelia—Jannitje—Mar. 12.

VAN ALE, Cornelis and Susanna—Johannis—May 13.

HOPPE, Abram and Antje—Jacob—Sep. 17.

1782

VAN DALSE, Hendrik—John—Jan. 6.
Wit: Jan Van Dalse.

WESTERVELT, John and Antje—Johannis, b. Dec. 21, 1781—Jan. 14.

VAN BLERKOM, Abram—Jannitje—Jan.
Wit: David Van Blerkom and wife.

ECKERSON, Edward—Jenny, b. Feb. 8—Feb. 17.
Wit: Jacob Eckerson and wife.
BOGERT, Casparus and Jannitje—Jenny, b. Feb. 11—Feb. 17.
BREVOORT, Samuel—Johannis, b. Feb. 25.
Wit: Johannis and Grietje Brevoort.
VERVELE, Gideon and Maria—Jannitje, b. Sep. 8—Oct. 13.
Wit: Cobus and Tittie Pilesvelt.
BLAUVELT, Pieter—Jannitje, b. May 17—June 6.
Wit: Barend Verseur and wife.
ALJEE, Abram and Jacomyntje—Jonathan, b. Dec. 4, 1781—Feb. 3.

1783 (?)

ACKERMAN, David G.—Jan—July 20.
Wit: Jan Terhuen and wife Trintie.

1783

GERRITSE, Hannis and Maria—Johannis—Feb. 2.
RATAN, Jacobus and Willempje—Jan—June 4.
Wit: Jan and Lea Zabriskie.
DAVIDS, Claas—Isaac—June 28.
Wit: Isaac Kiep and wife.
ZABRISKIE, Abram and Maria—Jelletje—Aug. 24.
Wit: Albert Zabriskie and wife.

1784 (?)

SESIE (or Lesie), Pieter—Isaac—Mar. 7.

1784

HOPPE, Gerrit—Jacomyntje—Feb. 11.
Wit: Jan Boskerk and wife.
BANTA, Jacob—Jan—May 30.
Wit: Jan Smith and wife.
DEMAREE, Samuel—Jacobus—Aug. 22.
Wit: Jacobus Perry and wife.
TERHUNE, Albert and Aaltje—Jacob—Aug. 22.
Wit: Jacob Zabriske and wife.
Bos, Dirk and Antje—Jan—Dec. 4.
Wit: Jan and Jantje Vanderbeek.

1785

LESIE, Johannis—Isaac—Mar. 20.
WESTERVELT, Jan and Rachel—Jacob—May 1.
Wit: Arie Westervelt and wife Geertje.
SPIER, David and Margrietje—John—July 3.
Wit: Pieter and Aaltje Van Order.
BOGERT, Steven and Maria—Jacobus and Petrus, b. July 8—July 24.
Wit: Petrus and Cathalyntje Westervelt: Jacobus and Cornelia
Bogert.
MAYBE, John and Leah—Johannis, b. June 28—July 24.
JERSEY, Pieter and Annatje—Jacob—Sep. 11.
Wit: Jacob and Anna Holstead.
ECKERSON, Thomas and Cornelia—Jannitje, b. Oct. 2.
Wit: Jacob Eckerson.

Post, Jacob and Sara—Jacob—Nov. 13.
Woertendyk, Reinier and Annatje—Jannitje, b. Nov. 26—Dec. 25.
Wit: Reinier and Jannitje Woertendyk.
Van Vlerkom, Peter and Jannitje—Jannitje, b. Nov. 24—Dec. 25.

1786

Hoppe, Gerrit Wm. and Grietje—Jonathan—Jan. 15.
Wit: Jan A. and Maria Hoppe.
Ackerman, Arie and Christina—Johannis, b. Jan. 18—Feb. 26.
Wit: Gerrit I. and Maria Hoppe.
Yurrie, Frederik and Jacomyntje—Jacobus, b. Sep. 1, 1783—Feb. 26.

1784

Van Blercom, Pieter and Christina—Jannitje, b. Nov. 4—Dec. 5.

1786

Waard, Pieter and Nancy—Jenneke, b. Apr. 1—Apr. 2.
Vande Beek, Johannis and Abigail—Jacob, b. Mar. 11—Apr. 2.
Wit: Jacob Vander Beek and wife.
Van Rype, Johannis and Geertje—John, b. Apr. 19—May 21.
Wit: Harme and Maria Van Rype.
Haring, Jan and Jannitje—Isaac, b. Apr. 20—June (?) Jan. (?) 4.
Wit: Jan and Elisabeth Haring.
Syoert, Isaac and Grietje—John, b. Apr. 23—June 4.
Wit: Abraham and Maria Zabriske.
Banner, James and Geesje—John De, b. May 28—July 2.
Wit: Jan, David and Angonietje Eckerson.
Rotan, Johannis and Jannitje—Johannis, b. July 10—July 23.

1787

Debow, Johannis and Margrietje—Jacomyntje, b. July 25, 1786—Jan. 12.
Wit: Jonathan and Catriena Traaphage.
Messeker, Lodewyk and Sara—Johannis—Apr. 15.
Wit: Hermanus and Elisabeth Van Zeyl.
Conklin, Lewis and Elisabeth—John, b. Apr. 7—May 20.
Wit: John and Catriena Conklin.
Zabriskie, Albert J. and Metje—Jacob, b. May 3—May 27.
Wit: Jacob A. and Sara Hoppe.
Ackerman, Abraham and Elisabeth—John—July 8.
Wit: John and Elisabeth Pulisvelt.
Eckerson, Jacob and Annaatje—Jan, July 26—Aug. 5.
Debaen, Andreas and Jannitje—Jacobus, b. July 25—Aug. 5.
Wit: Jacobus and Antje Debaen.
Miller, George and Hannah—Joost, b. July 15—Aug. 19.
Wit: Paulus and Doortie Vanderbeek.
Rotan, Daniel and Jannitje—Johannis, b. Aug. 9—Aug. 26.
Wit: John and Jannitje Rotan.
Eckerson, Thomas and Annaatje—John—Sep. 16.
Van Boskerk, Jan and Sara—Johannis, b. Aug. 12—Sep. 16.
Wit: Gerrit and Maria Hoppe.
More, John and Maria—Joseph—Sep. 16.

VAN DIEN, Albert and Polly—Johannis, b. Sep. 15—Oct. 7.
Wit: Jan and Molly Van Boskerk.

BERKHOF, Hendrik and Maria—Johannis—Dec. 30.

1788

POST, Johannis and Sara—Jacobus—Feb. 3.

ACKERMAN, David D. and Jannitje—Jannitje, b. Mar. 6—Mar. 23.
Wit: Jurrie and Maria Vanderbeek.

GOETSCHIUS, Joseph and Jannitje—Johannis Hendrikus—Apr. 20.

HOPPE, Nicasie and Maria—Jan, b. Mar. 19—Apr. 20.
Wit: Andreas and Elisabeth Hoppe.

HOPPE, Hendrik H. and Jacomyntje—Jan, b. May 31—June 22.
Wit: Rebecka Nagel.

BOGERT, Stephen and Fyke—Jacobus, b. June 23—Aug. 3.
Wit: Jacobus and Annaatje Aljee.

VAN VOORHESEN, Jan and Tryntje—Jacobus, b. July 13—Aug. 10.
Wit: Jacobus and Cornelia Bogert.

POOST, Abraham and Jannitje—Jannitje, b. Aug. 12—Aug. 31.

TERVEUR, Abraham and Elisabeth—Jacob, b. Sep. 11—Sep. 28.
Wit: Jacob and Marytje Debaen.

TAYLOR, William and Phebe—John, b. July 11—Oct. 19.

JANSE, Johannis and Fytje—Johannis, b. Nov. 18—Dec. 21.
Wit: Cornelius and Aaltje Haring.

1789

BERTOLF, Petrus and Angonietje—Jacobus, b. Oct. 18, 1788—Mar. 1.

ACKERMAN, Jacobus G. and Rachel—Jacob, b. Apr. 28—May 10.

ECKERSON, Cornelius and Catriena—Johannis, b. Mar. 30—June 7.
Wit: Johannis and Rachel Koning.

HARRIS, John and Grietje—Johannis, b. July 25—Aug. 9.
Wit: Johannis and Polly Gerritson.

FESYUOR, Jan W. and Wyntje—Johannis, b. Sep. 11—Nov. 1.
Wit: Jan and Lea Mebie.

1790

MUYSENER, Petrus and Peggy—Jacobus, b. Nov. 29, 1789—Jan. 24.
Wit: Jacobus and Lena Muysinger.

STRAAT, Jan and Susanna—John, b. Jan. 15—Jan. 31.
Wit: Jan and Maria Ryer.

RYER, Ryer and Maria—Jacobus, b. Feb. 26—Mar. 15.
Wit: Jacobus and Sara Woertendyck.

TERHUNE, Abraham and Soecke—Jacob, b. Mar. 2—Mar. 15.
Wit: Jacobus and Willempje Ratan.

BOGERT, Albert J. and Maria—Jacob—Jan. 31.
Wit: Jan J. Zabriskie; Jannitje Bogert.

BERDAN, Reinier and Geertje—Jan. b. July 22—Aug. 15.
Wit: Jan and Hendrikje Berdan.

ACKERMAN, Abraham and Salome—Johannis, b. Oct. 8—Dec. 12.

CERELLACH, John and Lena—John, b. Aug. 6—Dec. 12.
Wit: Battius and Grietje Schoenmaker.

1791

DEMAREST, Samuel C. and Catriena—Johannis, b. Dec. 25, 1790—Jan. 23.
Wit: Johannis and Elisabeth Ackerman.

MEBE, Isaac and Sara—Isaac, b. Jan. 10—Jan. 30.

GOETSCHIUS, Jan and Annaatje—Jacob, b. Dec. 30, 1790—Jan. 30.

YOUMENS, John and Elisabeth—John, b. Dec. 8, 1790—Jan. 30.

DEE, Salomon and Sally Dey—Jacob, b. Jan. 6—Feb. 16.

FERGUSON, Samuel and Jenny—Jannetje, b. Feb. 26—Apr. 17.

VANDERBEEK, Jacob and Annaatje—Jacobus, b. Mar. 26—Apr. 17.
Wit: Hendrik and Maria Frederikse.

ECKERSON, Nicholaas and Maria—Johannis, b. May 12—June 12.
Wit: Jan and Maria Eckerson.

LOZIER, John and Margrietje—Jannitje, b. Mar. 28—June 12.

WORTENDYK, Reinier and Annaatje—Johannis, b. Mar. 26—June 13.
Wit: Johannis and Maragrietje Fersyeur.

VANEMBURGH, Hendrik and Maria—John, b. June 28—July 17.
Wit: John and Lea Vanemburgh.

VALENTYNE, David and Rachel—Jacob, b. July 1—July 17.
Wit: Jacob and Liesje Valentyne.

CROUTER, Johannis and Maragrietje—Jacob and Aaltje, b. June 20—
July 24.
Wit: Jacob and Elisabeth Crouter.

VAN VLERKOM, Johannis and Elisabeth—Johannis, b. July 16—Aug. 14.
Wit: Johannis and Rebecka V. Vlerkom.

SLOT, Isaac and Lea—Jacob, b. Sep. 13—Oct. 23.

1792

THOMSON, Samuel and Jemima—Jacobus, b. Jan. 13—Feb. 26.

POST, Jacobus and Rachel—John—Feb. 26.

ACKERMAN, Arie and Christina—Jacomyntje—Feb. 26.

CLENDENNY, Walter and Osseltje—John—Apr. 10.

ACKERMAN, Johannis and Annatje—John, b. Mar. 18—Apr. 10.

HOPPE, Gerrit J. and Elisabeth—Jan, b. Mar. 3—Apr. 10.
Wit: Jan J. and Catriena Hoppe.

STORM, John and Maria—Isaac—Apr. 10.

VAN BLERKOM, John and Sara—Jannitje—Apr. 10.

TERHUNE, Abraham and Soecke—John, b. June 13—June 16.
Wit: Johannis and Abigael Vanderbeek.

JERSE, John and Maria—John, b. May 29—June 16.

CARLOGH, Nicolaas and Maria—Jacobus, b. Aug. 24—Sep. 30.
Wit: Jacobus and Sara Wannemaker.

FESHEUR, Abraham and Elisabeth—John, b. Sep. 18—Sep. 30.
Wit: Jaan and Aaltje Debaan.

QUACKENBOS, Barend and Catriena—Johannis, b. Mar. 5—Mar. 24.

HOPPE, Hendrik G. and Rachel—Jacob—Mar. 24.
Wit: Jacob J. and Wyntje Zabriske.

1793

DEBAAN, Andrias and Jannitje—Jacob, b. Dec. 4, 1792—Mar. 3.
Wit: Joost and Margrietje Debaan.

ECKERSON, Thomas and Cornelia—John, b. Nov. 21, 1792—Feb. 17.
Wit: John and Lena Eckerson.

DODS, James and Mary—Jacobus, b. Dec. 1—Feb. 17.
Wit: Abraham and Hannah Dator.

VAN WERT, Abraham and Ester—John—May 19.
Wit: John and Lea Van Wert.

BLAUVELT, Johannis and Metje—Johannis, b. May 14—June 9.
Wit: Jan and Maria Eckerson.

BLAUVELT, Daniel and Jannetje—John, b. Mar. 3—June 9.
Wit: John and Sara Van Vlerkom.

VOS, John and Jannitje—Jacobus, b. June 2—June 23.
Wit: Paulus and Grietje V. d. Beek.

DEMAREST, Catrina—Jannitje, b. May 9—June 30.
Wit: Andries and Jannetje Debaen.

McCALL, John and Geertrui—Jannetje, b. Mar. 3—July 7.

RYKER, Johannis and Jannetje—Jannetje, b. June 15—Aug. 4.
Wit: Albert and Jannetje Van Voorhesen.

DURIE, Pieter and Osseltje—Jan, b. June 19—July 28.
Wit: Jan and Rachel Durie.

RIDDENAAR, Coenraad and Elisabeth—John, b. July 31—Aug. 25.

BACKER, Jacob and Grietje—Jacob, b. June 14—Aug. 25.

BERDAN, Johannis and Maria—John, b. Aug. 30—Sep. 15.

LYDECKER, Gerrit and Martyntje—John, b. Oct. 10—Oct. 27.

CAMPBELL, John and Tietje—John, b. Nov. 13—Dec. 1.

1794

VAN SCHYVEN, William and Saartje—Johannis—Jan. 1.
Wit: Johannes and Jannetje Dremus.

DEBAAN, Jan and Aaltje—Jannitje, b. Feb. 10—Mar. 16.
Wit: Reinier Woertendyk; Jannitje Woertendyk.

ACKERMAN, Gerrit and Geertje—John, b. Apr. 10—May 4.
Wit: Hendrik and Jannetje Terhuen.

STRAAT, John and Soecke—Jacobus, b. Apr. 8—May 4.
Wit: Jacobus and Sara Wannemaker.

DEGROOT, Jacobus and Maria—Jacobus, b. Mar. 12—May 4.

ZABRISKIE, Albert and Lea—John, b. Apr. 20—May 4.
Wit: Cornelia Zabriskie.

EARLE, Edward and Abigail—John, b. Apr. 15—May —.
Wit: Gerrit and Jannitje Ackerman.

VAN VLERCOM, John and Sara—Isaac, b. May 17—June 22.

TEBOW, Peter and Susanna Te Bouw—Johannis, b. May 4—June 22.

HARING, David and Tryntje—Joost, b. May 17—July 6.
Wit: Joost and Tryntje Mebie.

FORGESON, Samuel and Jenny—Johannis, b. May 7—July 20.
Wit: Maria Myer.

VANORDEN, John and Tryntje—John, b. June 6—June 29.

BANTA, Hendrik and Maria—Jacob, b. Aug. 9—Aug. 31.
Wit: Jacob and Jannitje Stagg.

VAN HOUTEN, Jacobus and Elisabeth Berry—Jacobus, b. Apr. 3, 1793—Aug. 31.

VANDERBEEK, Coenradus and Annatje—Jurry, b. June 19—Aug. 10.
Wit: Jurry and Maria Vanderbeek.

HOPPE, Gerrit J. and Elisabeth—John, b. Sep. 6—Sep. 28.
Wit: Jan and Trientje Hoppe.

ECKERSON, Thomas and Susanna—Jacobus, b. Aug. 15—Sep. 21.
Wit: Jacobus and Sara Demarest.

HOPPE, Nicasie and Maria—Jacob, b. Sep. 17—Oct. 5.
Wit: Albert and Aaltje Terhune.

ACKERMAN, Daniel and Cathalyntje—Jannitje, b. Sep. 13—Oct. 5.
Wit: David and Jannitje Ackerman.

COOL, Abraham and Annatje—Isaac, b. Sep. 13—Oct. 5.
Wit: Isaac and Jannetje Cool.

POST, Jacob and Sara—John, b. Sep. 25—Oct. 19.

VAN DIEN, Albert and Maria—Jan Van Boskerk, b. Sep. 9—Oct. 26.
Wit: Jan and Geesje Van Boskerk.

TERHUNE, Abraham and Soecke—Jacob, b. Oct. 21—Nov. 16.
Wit: Jacobus and Willempje Ratan.

1795

BROWER, Petrus and Rachel—Johannis, b. Jan. 27—Feb. 12.
Wit: Johannis and Abigael V. D. Beek.

BLAUVELT, Isaack and Elisabeth—Jacobus, b. Jan. 18—Mar. 8.

VAN ALEN, Jan and Angonietje—Jacobus, b. Feb. 17—Mar. 29.
Wit: Jacobus and Cornelia Bogert.

HOPPE, Petrus and Elisabeth—Jonathan, b. Feb. 24—Apr. 6.

CHRISTOPHER, John and Aaltje—Jenny—Apr. 6.

ROMYN, Roelof—John, b. Mar. 28—May 24.

DEBAAN, Jacob and Osseltje—Jacob, b. May 2—May 17.

DERIST, Leashon and Elisabeth—Jacob, b. May 14—June 21.

V. D. BEEK, Harman and Antje—Jannetje, b. Aug. 28—Sep. 20.

VAN VOORHESEN, Jan and Tryntje—John, b. Oct. 2—Oct. 18.

SMITH, Abbott and Susanna—Jacobus, b. July 24—Oct. 25.
Wit: Jacobus and Catriena Smith.

DEE, Salomon and Sally—Isaak, b. Sep. 25—Oct. 27.

WOERTENDYK, Albert and Maragrietje—Jannitje, b. Nov. 10—Nov. 26.
Wit: Reinier and Jannitje Woertendyk.

CROUTER, Jacob and Maria—Jacobus, b. Nov. 30—Dec. 20.
Wit: Jacobus Crouter.

1796

FESYEUR, Cornelius and Jannetje—Jannitje, b. Dec. 15, 1795—Jan. 24.
Wit: Daniel and Jannitje Perry.

WATSON, Pieter and Maragrietje—John, b. Jan. 11—Feb. 7.
Wit: John and Maria Peeck.

DEGROOT, Jacobus and Maria—John, b. Feb. 23—Mar. 20.

DECKER, Cornelis and Nancy—John, b. Dec. 10, 1795—Apr. 3.

VANDIEN, Herman and Aaltje—Jan, b. July 15—Aug. 7.
Wit: Jan and Lea Zabriskie.

ROTAN, Jan and Jannitje—Jannitje, b. May 30—July 17.

HALDEROM, William and Catriena—Johannis, b. June 3—July 3.

CERELLAGH, Johannis and Leentje—Jure, b. Aug. 22—Sep. 25.
Wit: Jure and Sara Cerallagh.
BOGERT, John and Maragrietje—Jannitje, b. Nov. 27—Dec. 25.
Wit: David and Jannitje Ackerman.

1797

VAN WERT, Isaak and Elisabeth—John, b. Feb. 10—Mar. 19.
Wit: Matheus and Wyntje Barboro.
ECKER, Paulus and Maria—John, b. Feb. 7—Mar. 19.
ZABRISKE, Jacob J. and Wyntje—Jannitje, b. Mar. 4—Mar. 19.
Wit: Jacob and Jannitje Zabriske.
DURJEE, David and Geertje—Jannitje, b. July 23—Aug. 20.
DEBAAN, Carel and Sara—Jannitje, b. Nov. 6—Dec. 24.

1798

Bos, Lodewyk and Leentje—John, b. Jan. 22—Feb. 11.
Wit: John and Maria Ryer.
DURIE, Samuel and Catriena—Jannitje, b. Feb. 25—Apr. 1.
Wit: Andries and Jannitje Debaan.
HEMMION, Nicholaas and Lena—Johannis, b. Oct. 23, 1797—May 29.
WRIGHT, John and Abigail—Jannitje, b. Mar. 21—May 29.
TERHUNE, Albert and Lea—Isaac, b. June 13—June 20.
Wit: Pieter and Jacomyntje Stor.
ACKERMAN, Gerrit and Geertje—Jannitje, b. May 24—June 20.
Wit: Abraham and Maria Ratan.
SMIT, Jacobus and Catriena—Jannitje, b. Aug. 14—Aug. 26.
Wit: Daniel and Jannitje Perry.
VAN HOOPN, John and Elisabeth—John—Aug. 26.
DEGROOT, Jacobus and Maria—John, b. July 22—Aug. 26.
ZABRISKA, Albert and Aaltje—John, b. July 5—Sep. 9.
VANDERBEEK, Coenradus and Annatje—Jurie—Oct. 14.
TERHUNE, David and Catriena—Jannetje, b. Nov. 19—Dec. 9.
Wit: John and Antje Terhune.
LOZIER, Abraham and Annaatje—Jannetje, b. Sep. 15—Dec. 9.

1799

MOURESEN, Pieter and Grietje—Jacob, b. Nov. 12, 1798—Jan. 6.
BROUWER, John and Trientje—John, b. Dec. 3, 1798—Jan. 6.
Wit: John and Maria Jersey.
RATAN, Abraham and Wyntje—Jacobus, b. Dec. 14, 1798—Jan. 6.
Wit: Jacobus and Cornelia Bogert.
WESTERVELT, Albert and Maria—Joseph—Mar. 24.
DEMAREST, Syme and Maria—Johannis, b. Jan. 25—Mar. 24.
VALENTYNE, David and Rachel—John, b. Feb. 10—Apr. 14.
Wit: John Eckert and Rachel Valentine.
SHERWOOD, Isaak and Anna—Isaak, b. June 10—July 21.
VAN ORDEN, John and Tryntje—Jannetje, b. Sep. 9—Oct. 6.
BLAUVELT, Daniel and Annatje—Jannetje, b. Sep. 8—Oct. 6.
Wit: Cornelius and Jannetje Blauvelt.

Post, Jose and Aaltje—John, b. Aug. 3—Oct. 6.
 Wit: John and Catriena Storm.
See, John and Polly—John, b. Sep. 20—Oct. 13.
Doremus, Jacobus and Polly—Johannis, b. Dec. 2—Dec. 18.

1800

Van Houten, John and Antje—Isaak, b. Dec. 17, 1799—Jan. 5.
Scisco, William and Elisabeth—John, b. Jan. 17—Feb. 23.
Thompson, James—an adult—Apr. 13.
Dods, Thomas and Rachel—Jacobus, b. Mar. 19—Apr. 6.
 Wit: James and Maria Dods.
Blauvelt, Isaak and Sara—Jacobus, b. May 24—June 29.
 Wit: Jacobus and Rachel Blauvelt.
Bogert, Cornelius and Catrina—Johannis, b. Aug. 7—Aug. 31.
 Wit: Johannis and Maria Gerritson.
Goetsius, Piatus and Catriena—John, b. Sep. 3—Sep. 21.
Van Rypen, Cornelius and Elisabeth—John, b. Sep. 6—Oct. 2.
Ackerman, Abraham and Sarah—Jacomyntje, b. Oct. 5—Nov. 2.
Thew, James and Sarah—John, b. Oct. 9—Nov. 9.
Wortendyk, Cornelius—Johannis, b. Oct. 26—Nov. 9.
 Wit: Maria Wortendyk.
Degroot, Jacobus and Maria—Jannetje, b. Oct. 24—Nov. 30.
Stuart, Adolph—Jacobus, b. Oct. 17—Dec. 28.
 Wit: Jacobus and Jannetje Demarest.

1748

Dugrau, Jan and Lena—Janneke—Nov. 20.
 Wit: Anthony and Polly Van Blerkom.

1749

Terhuyn, David and Sara—Jan—Jan. 22.
 Wit: Cornelis and Lisabeth Bongaert.
Ackerman, Albert and Rachel—Jannitje—Apr. 23.
 Wit: Albert H. and Thelletje Zabriske.
Storm, Staets and Susan—Isaak—May 28.
 Wit: David and Marytje Hammon.
Dubaen, Jacob and Marytje—Jacobus—Aug. 15.
 Wit: Jacobus and Catryna Dubaen.
Zobriske, Albert Hen. and Thelletje—Jacob—Dec. 31.
 Wit: Jacob H. Zobriske; Lea Terhuyn, wife of Derrik.

1750

Ryer, Jan and Susanna—Jan, b. Feb. 12, 1750.
 Wit: Pieter and Rachel Mabe.
Hoppe, Willem and Antje—Jan—Mar. 20.
 Wit: Jan and Lisabeth Hoppe.
Van Blerkom, Jan G. and Vrouwtje—Jan—May 24.
 Wit: Jan and Lisabeth Hoppe.
Van Rype, Frederik and Antje—Johannis—Aug. 3.
 Wit: Hannis and Saartje Van Rype.
Banta, Abram and Annatje—Jakomyntje—Sep. 10.
 Wit: Thomas and Matje Ekker.
Van Voorhees, Cobus and Jannitje—Jacobus—Nov. 11.
 Wit: Gerrit D. and Lena Ackerman.
Bongaert, Cornelis and Lisabeth—Joost—Dec. 23.
 Wit: Albert J. Zabriske and Cornelia Bongaert.

1751

STORM, Abram and Aaltje—Johannis—Jan. 20.
Wit: Hannes and Lisabeth Ackerman.

ACKERMAN, Gerrit D. and Lena—Jannetje—May 12.
Wit: Jacobus and Jannitje Van Voorhees.

VAN BLERKOM, Hannes and Marytje—Johannis, b. July 7.
Wit: Abram and Rachel Van Gelder.

VANHOUTEN, Helmach—Janneke—Sep. 15.
Wit: Helmach D. and Antje Vanhoute.

———, ——— and ——— —Johannis—Oct. 6.
Wit: Pieter and Margrietje Dubouw.

1752

AMERMAN, Jan and Eva—Jacobus—Jan. 5.
Wit: Teunis and Cathalyntje Spier.

DUBAEN, Jacob and Marytje—Joost—May 17.
Wit: Ryer and Abigael Debouw.

MOORE, Jeremias and Lisabeth—Jannitje—June 21.
Wit: Andries Debouw.

BROUWER, Uldrick J. and Aaltje—Isaak—Aug. 9.
Wit: Isaac and Rachel Brouwer.

DUGRAU, Abel and Maaike—Jannitje, b. Sep. 14.
Wit: Hermanus and Jenneke Dugrau.

MYER, Abram and Catrientje—Jacob—Oct. 29.
Wit: Samuel and Marytje Brovoort.

HOPPE, Albert and Rachel—Jonathan—Oct. 29.
Wit: Hannes and Annatje Alyee.

1753

HOPPE, Willem and Antje—Jannitje—Jan. 21.
Wit: Hannes and Marytje Ryerse.

RUTAN, Abram and Saartje—Johannis—Jan. 28.
Wit: Arie and Lena Coerte.

ACKERMAN, Gerrit D. and Lena—Johannis—June 3.
Wit: Louwrens D. and Rachel Ackerman.

ACKERMAN, David D. and Annatje—Jannetje—July 1.
Wit: Hendrik and Cornelia Storm.

TERHUYN, Albert A. and Elisabeth—Johannis—July 1.
Wit: Cornelis and Rachel Duremes.

KROM, Hendrik and Grietje—Isaak—Dec. 2.
Wit: Isaak and Lena Conklin.

1754

BOOGERT, Albert and Machteld—Jacobus—Jan. 13.
Wit: Jacobus and Elsje Boogert.

BANTA, Jan H. and Grietje—Jan and Angonietje (twins)—July 28.
Wit: Jan J. and Wyntje Deryie; Jan B. and Maria Westervelt.

SLODT, Steven and Marietje—Johannis—Oct. 24.
Wit: Sam and Angonietje Sidman.

VANDER BEEK, Paulus and Annatje—Jannatje—Sep. 29.
Wit: Abram Ari and Lena Ackerman.

ZOBROWISKE, Steven and Tryntje—Jannetje—Dec. 8.
Wit: Jan J. and Aaltje Zobrowiske.

1755

VEEDER, Hermanus and Antje—Jacob—Jan. 1.
Wit: Hendrik C. and Maria Zobriske.

VANDERBEEK, Paulus I. and Rachel—Jannetje—Mar. 9.
Wit: Andries and Jannetje Dubouw.

BANTA, Jacob W. and Lena—Jan—Sep. 21.
Wit: Johannis H. and Lena Ackerman.

BALDEN, Steven and Antje—Joost—Sep. 28.
Wit: Joost and Carstyntje Zobriske.

1756

SYOURT, Willem and Trientje—Isaak—Apr. 25.
Wit: Roelof and Tryntje Westervelt.

DEBAEN, Petrus and Maria—Jacob, b. June 14—July 8.
Wit: David I. and Margrietje Demarest.

KOOL, Jacob and Rachel—Isaak, b. July 14—Sep. 5.
Wit: Lucas and Jannetje Kierstede.

VAN BLERKOM, Isaak and Saartje—Jannetje—Nov. 7.
Wit: Andries and Jannetje Debow.

ZABRISKE, Jacob and I. and Aaltje—Jan.—Dec. 25.
Wit: Jan and Aaltje Zabriske.

1757

VONCK, Pieter and Marytje—Jan, b. Jan. 15—Feb. —.
Wit: Hannes and Vrouwtje Van Schyven.

VANDERBEEK, Abram and Susanna—Jacob, b. July 26—Aug. —.
Wit: Femmetje Vanderbeek.

HOPPE, Hendrik and Wyntje—Jan.—Oct. 22.
Wit: Jan and Marietje Huysman.

1758

VANDERBEEK, Paulus and Rachel—Jacob—Jan. 14.
Wit: Isaak and Annatje Vanderbeek.

BANTA, Jan J. and Sara—Johannis—Feb. 5.
Wit: Sieba J. and Dievertje Banta.

MARCELESSE, Johannis and Belitje—Jacobus—Feb. 26.

DEY, Teunis and Hesther—Johannis, b. Apr. 16—May 14.
Wit: Isaak Schuyler and Antje Dey.

VAN RYPE, Simeon and Margriet—Jurrien—July 28.
Wit: Abram and Lea Cadmus.

WESTERVELT, Casparus and Martyntje—Johannis, b. July 26—Aug. 13.
Wit: Petrus and Cathalyntje Westervelt.

SLOT, Steven and Marytje—Isaak—Aug. 20.
Wit: Isack and Lisabeth Van Deuse.

DUBAEN, Jacob and Marytje—Johannis—Oct. 22.
Wit: Ned. and Antje Parrelman.

JENKENS, John and Jacomyntje—Jacobus, b. Sep. 26—Nov. 12.
Wit: Lambert and Lybe Laroi.

ACKERMAN, Willem and Grietje—Johannis—Nov. 12.
Wit: Johannes and Lisabeth Ackerman.

BOGERT, Lucas and Rachel—Jacobus—Nov. 19.
Wit: Cobus and Elsje Bogert.

1759

BALDWIN, Antje—Joost—Apr. 9.
Wit: Silvester and Machtel Earl.

VAN ZEYL, Hannes J.—Jakomyntje—May 24.
Wit: Hannes Van Zeyl and Lena Baremole.

RYERSE, Dirk and Lena—Jannetje—June 10.

VAN ZEYL, Hannes A. and Catriena—Johannis—July 1.
Wit: Hannes and Marytje Van Blerkom.

ALYEE, Isaak and Naatje—Joseph, b. June 27—July 22.
Wit: David and Rachel Eckerse.

RYERSE, Hannes F. and Marytje—Joris, b. July 3—Aug. 12.
Wit: Willem and Antje Hoppe.

LIVEASY, Robert and Annatje—Jacob—Nov. 10.
Wit: Roelof and Tryntje Westervelt.

VAN SCHYVE, Hannis and Vrouwtje—Jan—Dec. 2.
Wit: Niclaas and Samme Dumare.

VAN BLERCOM, Isaac and Sara—Johannis—Dec. 10.
Wit: Johannis and Marytje Van Blercom.

1760

VANHOREN, Lucas and Margrietje—Johannis—Feb. 17.
Wit: Gerrit and Catharina Blauvelt.

HOPPE, Abram and Rebecka—Jannetje—Mar. 22.
Wit: Hendrik A. and Wyntje Hoppe.

WESTERVELT, Casparus J. and Martyntje—Johannis, b. Apr. 10—Mar. 22.
Wit: Johannis and Eefje Westervelt.

ZABRISKE, Albert Jan and Geesje—Jan—May 8.
Wit: Jan Ja. and Aaltje Zabriske.

BENSEN, Matheus and Marytje—Hannes—Sep. 28.
Wit: Jan and Margrietje Berdan.

ZABRISKIE, Andries J. and Corstyntje—Jan—Sep. 28.
Wit: Jan and Aaltje Zobriske.

'FOCHI, Pieter and Maria—Jan—Nov. 16.
Wit: Jan and Catharina Fochi.

1761

VAN ES, Syme and Lisabeth—Jacob—Jan. 25.
Wit: Lisabeth and Abram Betolf.

HOPPE, Jan and Lisabeth—Jacob and Niklaas (twins)—Jan. 25.
Wit: Jan and Vrouwtje Van Blerkom; Gerrit and Cornelia Kip.

ZABRISKE, Andries and Lisabeth—Jannetje—Jan. 1.
Wit: Albert H. and Thelletje Zabriske.

RYERSE, Dirk F. and Betje—Johannis—Feb. 21.
Wit: Hannes Van Winkel.

HOPPE, Gerrit H. and Antje—Hendrik—Mar. 29.
Wit: Hendrik I. and Trintje Hoppe.

ACKERMAN, Willem and Grietje—Jacobus—Mar. 29.
Wit: Jacobus and Jannetje V. Voorhees.

STORM, Abram and Aaltje—Isaak, b. Apr. 17—May 10.
Wit: Isaac and Annatje Alyee.

---

¹Probably a corruption of Verseur.

BANTA, Jan H. and Grietje—Jacob—Nov. 1.
Wit: Jacob H. and Lena Banta.

HOPPE, Gerrit I. and Elsje—Jan—Dec. 6.
Wit: Jan and Geertje Hoppe.

V. DERBEEK, Abram C. and Saartje—Hannes—Dec. 20.
Wit: Hannes A. and Jacomyntje Ackerman.

1762

*TRAPHAGEN, Jonathan (or Hendrik) and Claartje—Jonathan—Jan. 1.
Wit: Willem Traphage and Rachel H. Hoppe.

HOPPE, Jan J. and Geertje—Jan—Jan. 24.
Wit: Jan A. and Lisabeth Hoppe.

BERDAN, Jan A. and Margrietje—Japick—Feb. 14.
Wit: Petrus and Jannetje Van Zeyl.

MABY, Hannes and Femmitje—Jacob, b. Mar. 28—May 2.
Wit: Abram and Brechje Dubaen.

CONKLIN, Isaak and Lena—Isaak—Oct. 17.
Wit: Samuel and Grietje Demare.

VANBLERKOM, Isaac and Sara—Johannis—Dec. 19.
Wit: Johannis and Marytje Vanblerkom.

1763

TERHUYN, Dirk and Lea—John—Oct. 9.
Wit: Jan A. and Lisabeth Hoppe.

†VOCHIE, Barend and Francyntje—Jannetje—Nov. 1.
Wit: Gerrit and Jannetje Blauvelt.

1764

ECKERSEN, Dirk—Jan—Jan. 29.
Wit: N. Springstien.

VAN ORDER, Jan and Jannitje—Johannis—Jan. 29.
Wit: Hannes and Trientje Van Zeyl.

DEPUU, Abram and Rachel—Johannis, b. Feb. 6—Mar. 18.
Wit: Johannis C. and Catriena Blauvelt.

ACKERMAN, Gerrit D. and Lena—Jacobus—Apr. 15.
Wit: Roelof and Tryntje Westervelt.

ACKERMAN, Hannes I. and Lena—Jacobus—Apr. 15.
Wit: Jacobus and Jannetje V. Voorhees.

SERVENT, Jacob and Trientje—Jacob—Apr. 15.
Wit: Jacob and Marytje Bogert.

SIDMAN, Samuel and Angonietje—John—Apr. 15.
Wit: Gerrit J. and Elsje Hoppe.

BERTOLF, Johannis and Wybrecht—Johannis, b. May 19—June 10.
Wit: Cobus H. and Lisabeth Bertolf.

VESIEUR, Willem and Lisabeth—Jan—June 7.
Wit: Jan and Catriena Veseur.

ACKERMAN, David J. and Nietje—Johannis—July 8.
Wit: Hannes and Lena Ackerman.

---

*The name *Jonathan* had been crossed out in the original and *Hendrik* put in its place, in a different handwriting.

†Probably a corruption of **Verseur.**

BONGAERT, Steven and Rachel—Jan—Sep. 16.
   Wit: Cobus and Cornelia Bongaert.
PERHEMEUS, Theodorus and Margrietje—Jacob, b. Sep. 14—Oct. 14.
STEGG, Isaac and Lena—Jacob—Oct. 28.
   Wit: David and Antje Banta.
TURNEUR, Jacobus and Grietje—Jacomyntje, b. Oct. 7—Nov. 4.
PARLEMAN, Jacobus—Jacobus, b. Dec. 9—Dec. 20.
   Wit: Andries and Jannitje Debouw.

1765

RYER, John and Susanna—Jannetje, b. Feb. 28—Mar. 31.
   Wit: Rynier and Jannetje Wortendyk.
PILESFELT, Hendrik and Cornelia—Johannis, b. Mar. 24—Apr. 14.
   Wit: Cobus and Tietje Pielesfelt.
ACKERMAN, Jan and Styntje—Johannis, b. Apr. 4—Apr. 28.
   Wit: Dom. B. and Lisabeth V. d. Linde.
ZABRISKE, Hendrik C. and Maria—Maria—Aug. 21.
   Wit: Andries and Lisabeth Zabriske.
BROUWER, Abram—Jannetje—Aug. 21.
   Wit: Andries and Jannetje Debouw.
PILESFELT, Jacobus and Tittie—Johannis—Nov. 3.
   Wit: Garrit and Tryntje Blauvelt.

1766

HOPPE, Albert and Rachel—Isaac—Jan. 12.
   Wit: Jan J. and Geertje Hoppe.
ACKERMAN, Gerrit J. and Rachel—Johannes—Mar. 16.
   Wit: Hannes and Lena Ackerman.
BLAUVELT, David and Rachel—Johannes, b. Apr. 19—May 10.
   Wit: Hannes and Catriena Blauvelt.
VANBLERKOM, David and Gerritje—Jan—June 1.
   Wit: Rachel Van Blerkom.
ZABRISKE, Jacob J. and Jannetje—Jan—Sep. 14.
   Wit: Andries and Tiena Zobriske.
STEGG, Isaac and Lena—Isaac—Sep. 21.
   Wit: Gerrit J. and Rachel Ackerman.
McDANNEL, Cornelis and Catriena—Jacob—Sep. 7.
   Wit: Jacob Eckerson.
VAN BLERKOM, David and Elisabeth—Jacomyntje—Dec. 18.
   Wit: David A. and Jacomyntje Ackerman.

1767

DUBAEN, Jacob and Rachel—Jacob, Rachel, b. Jan. 26—Feb. 15.
   Wit: Jacob B. and Sara Coel; Abram and Brechje Dubaen.
HOPPE, Andries A. and Lisabeth—Jacob—Mar. 22.
   Wit: Jacob and Saartje Hoppe.
LEVISIE, Paulus and Elisabeth—Jan—Mar. 29.
   Wit: Jan and Jannitje Vanderbeek.
WARD, Samuel and Abigael—Jones—Mar. 29.
   Wit: Pieter H. and Jannitje Vanblerkom.

BANTA, Cornelis A. and Maria—Joseph, b. Aug. 15—Sep. 6.
Wit: Isaac and Annatje Alyee.

VAN BLERKOM, David and Lisabeth—Jannetje—Sep. 27.
Wit: Pieter Maybe, Jr., and wife.

1768

LUTKENS, Pieter and Annatje—Jan—Feb. 21.
Wit: Jan and Belitje Doremus.

PILESVELT, Andries and Cornelia—Johannes, b. Jan. 26—Mar. 6.
Wit: Hannes and Tryntje Winter.

COCKROW, Niklaas and Pietertje—Jannetje—Mar. 13.
Wit: Jacob and Marytje Bogert.

HUNTER, Robert and Mollie—Jannetje—Mar. 27.
Wit: Jacobus and Titie Pilesvelt.

ACKERMAN, David D. and Jannetje—Jannetje—Mar. 27.
Wit: Jurjen and Marytje V. derbeek.

DUBAEN, Jacob and Marytje—Jacob—May 15.
Wit: Jan and Grietje Straet.

ACKERMAN, Gerrit J. and Rachel—Johannes—Aug. 28.
Wit: Johannes J. and Lena Ackerman.

TRAPHAGE, Hendrik and Claartje—Jacobus—Aug. 28.
Wit: Jan H. and Fytje Hoppe .

ALYEE, Isaac and Annatje—Jan, b. June 3—Aug. 28.
Wit: Jan and Grietje Banta.

BLAUVELT, Gerrit and Annatje—Jannetje, b. Aug. 2—Sep. 19.
Wit: Christiaan and Jannetje Blauvelt.

ACKERMAN, Johannis and Lena—Johannis—Oct. 23.
Wit: Abram J. and Brechje Ackerman.

ZOBRISKE, Andries J. and Carstina—Jan—Dec. 19.
Wit: Jan and Aaltje Zobriske.

TOIRS, Lourens and Lisabeth—Jan—Dec. 25.
Wit: Jan and Styntje Ackerman.

1769

PARRELMAN, Han Jurry and Maria—Isaac—Sep. 10.
Wit: Maurits Mourusse and Annatje Debow.

ACKERMAN, Arie and Marytje—Johannes, b. Apr. 26—May 20.
Wit: Hannes A. and Jacomyntje Ackerman.

1749

ACKERMAN, Gerrit D. and Lena—Lisabeth—Aug. 27.
Wit: Pieter and Lisabeth Post.

1750

ACKERMAN, Abram I. and Hester—Lisabeth—Mar. 20.
Wit: Hannes and Lisabeth Ackerman.

VAN BLERKOM, Pieter and Susanna—Lisabeth—Apr. 15.
Wit: Gerrit and Elsje Hoppe.

SEDMAN, Samme and Angonietje—Lisabeth—Nov. 11.
Wit: Isaak I. and Lisabeth Van Deuse.

1752

JURRIKSE, Harme and Jannetje—Lisabeth—Mar. 8.
Wit: Samuel and Rebecka Bos.

TOERS, Hannes and Geertje—Lea—Feb. 9.
Wit: Abram C. Ackerman and Francyntje Toers.

ZABRISKE, Jacob C. and Lena—Lea—July 29.
Wit: Andries C. and Lisabeth Zabriske.

1754

Pyper, David—Lodewyk—Jan.——
Wit: Hannes and Vrouwtje Van Schyve.
Syourt, Joost and Lidea—Lewis—Nov. 25.
Wit: Lewis and Hatty Conklin.

1755

Earl, Sylvester and Machtel—Lisabeth—Aug. 17.
Wit: Albert J. and Geertje Zobriskie.
Banta, Abram and Annatje—Lea—Sep. 14.
Wit: Jan and Grietje Banta.
Meyer, Hannes M. and Lea—Lena—Nov. 4.
Wit: Adolf and Lena Meyer.
Ackerman, Hannes H. and Lena—Lisabeth—Nov. 16.
Wit: Hannes and Lisabeth Ackerman.

1756

Berry, Philip—Lena—Jan. 5.
Wit: Simeon and Lisabeth Van Winkel.
Macelese, Ceel and Elisabeth—Janneke, b. Oct. 18—Nov. 7.
Wit: Pieter and Janneke Macelese.
Demarest, Cornelis and Marytje—Lisabeth—Nov. 7.
Wit: Hannes and Lisabeth Ackerman.

1759

Devenpoort, Omphre and Willemina—Lea—Jan. 31.
Wit: Leendert and Lea Kool.
V. Blerkom, Hermanus and Aaltje—Lena—Apr. 14.
Wit: Hannes H. and Lena Ackerman.

1761

Slot, Steven and Marritje—Lisabeth—Jan. 25.
Wit: Isaak and Lisabeth Van Deuse.
Van Zeyl, Hans and Catharina—Lena, b. Jan. 27—Feb. 1.
Wit: Hendrik Ryke and Lena Baremole.
Toers, Louwrens and Lisabeth—Lena—July 5.
Wit: Hannes and Lena Van Houte.

1762

Bogert, Cornelis and Lisabeth—Lisabeth—Mar. 8.
Wit: Klaas and Rachel Zobriske.

1763

Laroi, Hannes and Margrietje—Lena, b. Mar. 20—Apr. 17.
Wit: Gerrit and Lena Ackerman.
Heaton, Richard and Maria—Lisabeth, b. Apr. 14—May 7.
Wit: Samuel P. and Lena Dumare.

1765

Vanhoren, Cornelis C. and Geesje—Lisabeth, b. Oct. 10—Nov. 10.
Wit: Cornelis and Lisabeth Vanhoren.

1766

Jurlie (or Surlie), James and Marytje—Lourens—Mar. 30.
Wit: Teunis and Grietje Helm.
Vandien, Thomas and Polly—Lisabeth—Mar. 23.
Wit: Cornelis and Lisabeth Bogert.
Dubaen, Jacob and Marytje—Lisabeth—June 1.
Wit: Dirk and Lisabeth Vanhoren.

1767 KROM, Teunis and Catriena - Lisabeth, b. Feb 22 - Apr. 19.
Wit: Cornelis and Catrina Macdannel.

1769 MICKLER, Hans and Grietje - Lisabeth - Feb. 5.
Wit: Pieter and Lisabeth Swin.
POST, Hannes and Trientje - Lisabeth - Dec. 3.
Wit: Cobus and Metje Post.

1770 DERYIE, Jan P. and Jannitje - Lisabeth - Feb. 4.
Wit: Hannes and Lisabeth Blauvelt.
COCKROW, Niklaas and Pietertje - Lisabeth - Mar. 25.
Wit: Nates and Lisabeth Steger.
V. BLERKOM, David J. and Geritje - Lisabeth - Sep. 20.
Wit: Lucas and Lisabeth Vanblerkom.
ZOBRISKE, Jacob H. and Wyntje - Lisabeth - Dec. 2.
Wit: Albert and Lisabeth Terhuyn.

1771 ACKERMAN, Albert G. and Antje - Lena - June 23.
Wit: Gerrit and Lena Ackerman.
DUMAREE, Cornelis I. and Grietje - Lea - Aug. 4.
DAVIS, Niklaes and Marytje - Lisabeth - Aug. 25.
Wit: Hannes J. and Rebecka Van Blerkom.
ZABRISKIE, Christiaan J. and Marytje - Maria - Apr. 15.
Wit: Steve and Titje Terhune.

1773 BROUWER, Abram D. and Antje - Lea - June 20.
Wit: Jan W. and Lea Van Voorhese.

1774 Hoppe, Hendrik J. and Aaltje - Lisabeth - May 8.
Wit: Jan and Lisabeth Hoppe.
TRAPHAGE, Hendrik - Marytje - May 29.
Wit: Jurry and Marytje Vanderbeek.
SWIN, Pieter and Elisabeth - Marytje - May 29.
Wit: Jan and Jannetje Van Orden.

1776 V. DERBEEK, Hannes and Ebbie - Lea - Jan 28.
Wit: Hendrik and Polly Terhune.
BANTA, Angenietje - Lisabeth Bogert, b. Apr. 17 - May 12.
Wit: Jan and Grietje Banta; Hendrik and Grietje Banta.

1778 ZOBRISKE, Abram A. and Marytje - Lisabeth - Sep. 13.
Wit: Albert A. and Betje Terhuyn.

1779 WESTERVELT, Johannes and Antje - Lucas, b. May 28 - July 25.
Wit: Cornelis L. and Lisabeth Bogert.
VALENTINE, Jacob and Grietje - Lisabeth - Sep. 19.

1780 BOGERT, Casparus and Jennetje - Lisabeth - May 15.
Wit: Belkje Bogert.

1783 V. HOOREN, Daniel - Lisabeth - Feb. 20.

1784 VANDEBEEK, Johannis - Lea - Apr. 15.
Wit: Hendrik Hoppe and wife.
ACKERMAN, David - Lea - Apr. 25.
LAZIER, Abram - Lisabeth - Aug. 22.

1785
HOPPE, Gerrit—Elisabeth—Apr. 10.
Wit: Hendrik Hoppe and wife.
HOPPE, Andries and Tryntje—Lea—May 1.
Wit: Hendrik and Rachel Terhune.
BAMPER, Jacob and Antje—Lodewyk Marcelis—May 16.
Wit: John and Anne Barberrier.
EARLE, Edward and Abigail—Lena—Oct. 23.
Wit: Abraham and Margrietje Rotan.

1786
BANTA, Hendrik and Maria—Lena, b. May 3—May 21.
Wit: Jacob Stagg and Sara Bogert.
ACKERMAN, Johannis and Elisabeth—Lena, b. May 19—June 26.
Wit: Lena Ackerman.

1788
TOERS, Arie and Rachel—Louwrens, b. June 2—June 29.

1789
VAN VOORHEESEN, Abraham and Angonietje—Lea, b. Sep. 10—Oct. 25.
Wit: Jan and Lea Van Voorheesen.

1792
MESSEKER, Lodewyk and Sara—Lodewyk, b. Jan. 29—Feb. 26.
JENKINS, Lambert and Annatje—Lena, b. Feb. 15—Apr. 10.

1793
PERRY, John and Charity—Lidea, b. Sep. 8—Oct. 13.

1794
ACKERMAN, Marmeduck and Lena—Lena, b. Aug. 6—Aug. 31.
STOR, Jacob and Geesje—Lea, b. Aug. 4—Sep. 14.
Wit: Gerrit Post and Anna Van Rype.

1795
TERHUUN, Hendrik and Tryntje—Lea, b. Feb. 22—Mar. 15.
Wit: Jan and Lea Van Imburg.
COERTEN, John and Catrina—Lena, b. Apr. 15—May 17.
Wit: Leuwer (Lewis?) and Lena Winter.

1796
TERHUNE, Andrias and Antje—Lea, b. Feb. 2—Feb. 7.
Wit: Johannis and Abigail Vanderbeek.

1797
MEBE, Abraham and Maria—Lea, b. Jan. 13—Mar. 19.
ECKERSON, Gerrit and Annaatje—Lea, b. Nov. 1—Nov. 26.

1798
HALDEROM, William and Catriena—Lena, b. Feb. 28—Apr. 1.
Wit: Niclaas and Lena Halderom.
TERHUNE, Abraham and Soeke—Lea, b. June 24—Aug. 26.
Wit: Hendrik and Aaltje Hopper.
MESSEKER, Lodewyk and Sara—Lena—Dec. 9.

1799
ECKER, Abraham and Tryntje—Lea, b. Mar. 22—Apr. 14.
MEBE, Pieter and Jannetje—Lea, b. Apr. 30—July 7.
TOERS, Jacob and Aaltje—Lourens, b. Oct. 6—Nov. 3.

1800
HOPPER, Hendrik and Charrette—Lewis, b. July 10—July 27.

1749

VAN DEUSE, Isaak and Lisabeth—Maria— Aug. 13.
Wit: Cobus and Rebecka Laroe.

WANNEMAKER, Hendrik and Lisabeth—Margrietje—Sep. 17.
Wit: Coenraad and Margriet Vredriks.

1751

RUTAN, Daniel D. and Susan—Marytje—June 14.
Wit: Hannes and Francyntje Brikker.

ODEL, Benjamin and Nelli—Maria—Aug. 25.
Wit: Isaac and Lena Conkling.

MYER, Hannes and Lena—Marytje—Aug. 25.
Wit: Samuel and Marytje Bravoo.

ZABRISKE, Jacob I. and Aaltje—Maria—Feb. 10.
Wit: Albertus and Anna Maria Terhuyn.

——, —— and —— —Marytje—Sept. 29.
Wit: Bille and Maragrietje Ginckins.

HOPPE, Gerrit and Elsje—Marytje—Oct. 20.
Wit: Abram and Marytje Lasier.

1752

VAN ZEYL, Peter and Lena—Marytje and Lena (twins)—Jan. 5.
Wit: Hendrik and Marytje Messeker; Isack and Lena Conkling.

TERHUYN, Albert A. and Lisabeth—Maria—Jan. 26.
Wit: Albertus and Anna Maria Terhuyn.

TERHUYN, Dirk A. and Lea—Maria—Sep. 24.
Wit: The same as above.

WANNEMAKER, Pieter D. and Marytje—Margrieta—Sep. 24.
Wit: Adolf Schyoert and Margrieta Schyoert.

1753

ALYEE, Cobus and Annatje—Margrieta—Mar. 4.
Wit: Pieter and Margrieta Alyee.

ZABRISKE, Albert C. and Aaltje—Marytje—Oct. 1.
Wit: Jacob C. and Lena Zabriske.

BANTA, Jacob and Lena—Maria—Dec. 23.
Wit: Cornelis and Lidea Myer.

1754

STORM, Abram and Aaltje—Maria—Jan. 13.
Wit: Cornelis and Marytje Demarest.

GRAU, Hermanus D. and Jannike—Geertrui—Apr. 14.
Wit: Joris and Antje Stegg.

BROUWER, Uldrick and Aaltje—Marytje—Apr. 14.
Wit: Hannes and Jacomyntje Ackerman.

ZOBRISKE, Jacob H. and Wyntje—Marytje—Apr. 15.
Wit: Albertus and Marytje Terhuyn.

HOPPE, Albert and Rachel—Margrietje—Oct. 13.
Wit: Stefanus and Santje Terhuyn.

PARLMAN, Ned D. and Antje—Margriet—Nov. 25.
Wit: Steve and Maritje Slot.

1755

HOPPE, Willem and Antje—Maria, b. Apr. 29—May 11.
Wit: Jacob Jan Zobriske and Marytje Hoppe.

BONGAERT, Cornelis and Lisabeth—Martyntje—June 15.
Wit: Abram and Martyntje Haring.

V. BLERKOM, Hermanus and Aaltje—Margrietje—Oct. 12.
Wit: Louwrens Ackerman and Grietje Van Voorhees.
MEYER, Marcus and Willemyntje—Maria—Nov. 16.

1756

ACKERMAN, Johannis Ar. and Jacomyntje—Marytje—Feb. 1.
Wit: Jurry and Marytje Vanderbeek.
BONGAERT, Albert C. and Sara C.—Maria, b. Jan. 17—Feb. 15.
Wit: Abram A. and Marytje Haring.
SIDMAN, Samuel and Angonietje—Marytje, b. Feb. 4—Mar. 7.
Wit: Benjamin and Wybrech Demare.
ZABRISKE, Hendrik and Maria—Martyntje—May 30.
Wit: Abram and Martyntje Haring.
ACKERMAN, Albert and Rachel—Metje—Dec. 25.
Wit: Abram G. Ackerman and Lena Van Winkel.

1757

ECKER, Thomas and Marytje—Maria, b. Jan. 9—Jan. 16.
Wit: Cornelis and Matje Demarest.

1759

TOERS, Lourens and Lisabeth—Marytje—Jan. 21.
Wit: Niklaas and Mettie Volk.
PECKER, Jacob and Elisabeth—Maria—May 20.
Wit: Hannes and Marytje Vanblerkom.
MOURESE, Dirk and Rachel—Marytje—May 3.
Wit: Pieter and Marytje Mourese.
LODEWYK, Hendrik and Rosina—Maria—Sep. 9.
Wit: Christiaen and Maria Caef.
RYERSE, Joris F. and Maria—Marte—Sep. 23.
Wit: Marte F. and Antje Ryerse.
TERHUYN, Abram and Marytje—Maria—Dec. 20.
Wit: Jacob I. and Aaltje Zabriske.

1760

ALYEE, Albert and Maria—Maria, b. Feb. 20—Mar. 9.
Wit: Isack and Annatje Alyee.
MABE, Pieter, Jr. and Jannitje—Myndert, b. Feb. 19—Mar. 29.
Wit: Myndert and Lena Hogenkamp.

1763

JENKINS, Willem and Margriet—Maria, b. Jan. 20—Feb. 29.
Wit: Jacob and Marytje Kogh.
HOPPE, Willem and Antje—Magdalena, b. Apr. 2—Apr. 27.
Wit: Abram and Rebecka Hoppe.

1764

ZABRISKE, Jacob J. and Jannitje—Marytje—Apr. 15.
Wit: Hannes and Marytje Brevoort.
MYER, Hannes C. and Saartje—Maria—Apr. 15.
Wit: Thomas and Marytje Eckersen.

1765

HUYLER, Cornelia—Margrietje—Jan. 13.
Wit: Jan and Grietje Banta.

PIELISFELT, Willem and Lisabeth—Maria, b. Mar. 15—Apr. 14.
Wit: Christiaan and Marytje Pilesfelt.

BRUYN, Coenraad and Antje—Marytje, b. May 7—May 26.
Wit: Abram and Marytje Ackerman.

1762

ZOBRISKE, Hendrik C. and Maria—Margrietje—Mar. 20.
Wit: Isaak and Margrietje Blance.

SCHOEMAKER, Lodewyk and Catryn—Anna Margriet—June 27.
Wit: Dirk Wannemaker and Margriet Milrien.

ECKERSEN, Dirk and Maria—Maritje—Sep. 5.
Wit: Cobus and Ariaantje Springstien.

VAN SCHYVE, Hans and Vrouwtje—Maria—Dec. 19.
Wit: Joseph and Maria Fits.

1763

V. DER VOORT, David and Brechje—Maria, b. Feb. 27—June 12.

1765

VESEUR, Barend and Sientje—Maria—Dec. 28.
Wit: Pieter and Maria Vosuer.

1766

TERHUYN, Abram and Marytje—Maria—Mar. 16.
Wit: Jacob J. and Aaltje Zobriske.

*WENDYK, Reinier and Jannitje—Maria, b. Mar. 25—Apr. 6.
Wit: Pieter and Maria Veseur.

WESTERVELT, Johannis and Antje—Maria—July 13.
Wit: Abram and Marytje Terhuyn.

HOGENKAMP, Jan and Elisabeth—Myndert, b. Aug. 29—Sep. 21.
Wit: Myndert and Helena Hogenkamp.

V. D. BEEK, Pàulus and Rachel—Marytje—Sep. 14.
Wit: Jacob and Marytje Ryerson.

RYERSE, Ryer J. and Lisabeth—Maria—Sep. 14.
Wit: Cathalyntje and Johannis R. Ryerse.

DOBS, Willem and Rachel—Maria—Sep. 14.
Wit: Willem and Maria Rutan.

1767

ECKERSEN, David and Angonietje—Maria—Feb. 25.
Wit: Thomas and Maria Eckersen.

PILESFELT, Hendrik and Cornelia—Maria—Mar. 22.

SLOT, Steven and Marietje—Marytje—June 7.
Wit: Christiaan and Marietje Van Deuse.

ODEL, Hendrik and Marytje—Marytje—Sep. 27.
Wit: Joseph and Ariaantje Wessels.

MYER, Cornelis M. and Ariaantje—Mettie—Nov. 5.
Wit: Niklaas and Mettie Volk.

HELM, Samuel and Tryntje—Marte—Dec. 6.

---

*Probably Wortendyk.

1768

PIELESFELT, Coenraad and Eva—Margrietje, b. Jan. 2—Mar. 6.
Wit: Jan and Grietje Huyler.
PARRELMAN, Cobus and Antje—Margrieta—June 5.
Wit: Samuel and Rebecka Bos.

1769

HOPPE, Albert and Rachel—Marytje—Jan. 29.
Wit: Abram and Marytje Ackerman.
VAN BLERKOM, David J. and Lisabeth—Marytje—Jan 29.
Wit: Abram and Maritje Maebie.
PIETERSE, Niklaas and Maria—Maria, b. Jan. 21—Feb. 19.
Wit: Jacob and Lena Myer.
BONGAART, Andries and Trientje—Maria—Feb. 19.
Wit: Samuel and Lea Terhuyn.
BANTA, Cornelis A. and Maria—Maria—Dec. 31.
Wit: Isaak and Annatje Alyee.

1770

BANTA, Samuel and Elisabeth—Maria, b. Jan. 23—Feb. 18.
Wit: Thomas and Maria Eckerson.
DUBAEN, Jacob and Marytje—Margrietje—July 29.
Wit: Samuel and Rebecka Bos.
DOBS, William and Rachel—Maria—Dec. 30.
Wit: Willem and Vroutje Rutan.

1771

LAROI, Hannes and Grietje—Maria—Jan. 13.
Wit: Albert W. and Marytje Van Voorheese.
HOPPE, Andries A. and Lisabeth—Micle—Feb. 24.
Wit: Micle and Saartje Post.
POST, Pieter P. and Neesje—Metje—Mar. 17.
Wit: Cobus C. and Mettie Post.
WALDEROM, Barend and Lena—Margrietje, b. Feb. 15—Apr. 1.
Wit: Abram and Grietje Blauvelt.
VERSEUR, Barend and Francyntje—Magdalena—Apr. 28.
Wit: Hannes and Magdalena Verseur.
VANDERBEEK, Jurry and Marytje—Maria—May 19.
Wit: Hannes A. and Jacomyntje Ackerman.
TRAPHAGE, Jonathan and Catriena—Maria, b. May 10—June 2.
Wit: Jacob and Maria Cogh.
WOERTENDYK, Frederik and Majere—Majere, b. June 26—July 21.
ECKERSEN, Jan and Marytje—Mettie—Sep. 1.
Wit: Cornelis and Ariaantje Myer.
VANHOREN, Hannes B. and Rachel—Margrietje, b. Aug. 20—Sep. 15.
Wit: Gerrit and Grietje Gerritse.
BANTA, Jacob A. and Rachel—Maria, b. Nov. 3—Dec. 1.
Wit: Cornelis and Maria Smit.

1772

MYER, Cornelis M. and Ariaantje—Marte—Jan. 5.
Wit: Marte J. and Lisabeth Myer.

TRAPHAGE, Hendrick and Willemyntje—Mettie—Mar. 8.
Wit: Dirk and Cornelia Dykman.
ECKERSON, Thomas T. and Cornelias—Maria—Aug. 23.
Wit: Thomas and Maria Eckerson.
POURHEMIUS, Johannis and Maria—Margrietje—Sep. 13.
Wit: Theodore and Margrietje Pourhemius.
BOGERT, Cobus and Cornelia—Marytje—Dec. 25.
Wit: Hendrik and Marytje Oldes.

1773

DUMAREE, Cornelis J.—Maria, b. Feb. 15—Mar. 21.
Wit: Thomas Eckerson.
LAROI, Jacobus S. and Annatje—Marietje—Nov. 7.
Wit: Gerrit A. and Margriet Gerritse.
VAN RYPE, Harme and Maria—Maria—Dec. 25.
Wit: Cobus and Annatje Perry.

1774

ZOBRISKE, Hendrik I. and Willempje—Magdalena—Feb. 6.
Wit: Cornelis C. and Lena Bogert.
ACKERMAN, David D. and Jannitje—Margrietje—July 10.
Wit: Abram D. and Margrietje Ackerman.
BLAUVELT, Christiaen and Cathalyntje—Margrietje—Aug. 7.
Wit: Willem and Grietje Halderom.

1775

GUTSIUS, Jan - Maria - Jan. 7.
Wit: Adam Beatie and wife.
ECKERSEN, Jan and Marytje - Maria, b. Jan. 3 - Jan. 22.
Wit: Coenradus and Maria Storm.
ACKERMAN, Arie and Marytje - Margrietje, b. July 2 - Aug. 20.
Wit: Willem and Margrietje Halderom.
BANTA, Jan C. and Annatje - Maria, b. Aug. 8 - Sep. 17.
Wit: Richard and Maria Eathen.
WANNEMAKER, Dirk - Maria - Sep. 17.
wit: Coenraad C. and Marytje Wannemaker.
DEY, Isaac and Syntje - Maria - Dec. 3.

1776

RUTAN, Jacob W. and Grietje - Maria - Jan. 28.
Wit: Niklaas and Marietje Pieterse.

1778

HOPPE, Jan J. and Jannitje - Maria - May 5.
Wit: Abram A. and Femmitje Boskerck.

1776

RUTAN, David W. and Aaltje - Maria, b. July 11 - July 28.
Wit: Willem and Rachel Dobs.
V. BLERKOM, David J. and Gerritje - Martynus - Aug. 25.
Wit: Jan and Lisabeth Fliereboom.
BAMPER, Jacob and Antje - Margrieta Helena, b. Oct. 17 - Nov. 14.
Wit: Jan and Lisabeth Fliereboom.
POST, Jacob and Saartje - Maria - Nov. 15.

1779
ACKERMAN, Hannes G. and Lisabeth—Maria—Apr. 5.
  Wit: Harme and Maria Van Rype.
HARRISON, James and Mary—Margrit—Apr. 5.

1780
SLOT, Isaac and Lea—Maritje—Sep. 24.
  Wit: Steven and Marietje Slot.

1781
DEMAREE, Thomas and Lena—Maria, b. July 20—Aug. 19.
ECKER, Cornelis—Maria—Nov. 6.
  Wit: Isaak and Jacomyntje Blauvelt.
TERHUYN, Albert and Aaltje—Maria, b. June 3—June 12.
  Wit: Abram and Marytje Terhuyn.

1782
HOPPE, Jan W. and Annatje—Marytje Martyntje, b. Jan 7, 1781—Feb. 10.
HOPPE, Jan and Maria—Maria—May 11.
VANDIEN, Thomas and Pollie—Maria—Dec. 20.
  Wit: Jan Zabriskie.

1783
VAN BLERCOM, Johannis—Maria—Feb. 16.
HOPPE, Hendrik—Metje—Mar. 14.
  Wit: Hendrik Terhune and wife.

1784
———, ———— and ———— —Maria—May 30.
BROUWER, Jacob—Maria—June 27.
STORM, Isaac-Metje-June 27.
  Wit: Jac Ecker and Wife.
LOZIER, Jan-Mary-Aug 8.

KOOL, Abram—Grietje—Sep. 5
VAN HOUTEN, Petrus and Marritje Onderdonck—Maria—Sep. 19.
  Wit: Petrus and Maritje Van Houten.
DOREMES, David and Lea—Margrietje, b. Sep. 2—Dec. 2.
  Wit: Johannis and Grietje Prevoo.

1785
HOPPER, Gerrit A. and Cathalyntje—Marytje—Mar. 6.
WOERTENDYK, Vrerik—Mary (?)—May 1.
  Wit: Cornelis Smit and wife.
HALDRUM, Hendrik—Maria—May 1.
HOPPEN, Gerrit and Antje—Maria—May 5.
MYER, Jacob and Abigail-Maria, b. Aug. 17-Sep. 25.
  Wit: Hendrik and Maria Riddenaar.

1786
WILSON, Albert and Maria-Maria-Feb. 26.
  Wit: Gerrit Jinkens and Elisabeth Stagg.
SERVENT, Jan and Margrietje-Martha, b. Feb 21-Apr 9.
  Wit: Johannis and Rebecka Fesyeur.
BLAUVELT, Daniel and Jannetje-Maria, b. Mar 8-Apr 16.
  Wit: Gerrit B. and Jannetje Ackerman.

1789

BENSEN, Albert and Jannetje—Matheus, b. Jan. 28—Feb. 8.
Wit: John and Maritje Van Vlercom.

VRERICKSON, Isaak and Maria—Maria, b. Jan. 7—Feb. 8.
Wit: Joseph Horn.

POST, Jacobus and Rachel—Metje, b. Jan. 2—Mar. 1.

DEMAREST, Samuel and Catriena—Maria, b. Feb. 9—Mar. 1.
Wit: Harmen and Maria Van Rypen.

ECKERSON, Petrus and Annatje—Maragrietje—Apr. 5.
Wit: Johannis and Maragrietje Crouter.

DEMAREST, Daniel and Maria—Maria, b. Feb. 15—June 7.

ACKERMAN, Gerrit G. and Jannetje—Maria, b. July 12—Aug. 9.
Wit: Petrus and Elisabeth Poelisfelt.

1790

STEEL, Matheus and Elisabeth—Maria—Jan. 24.
Wit: Albert and Jannetje Benson.

HOPPE, Jan A. and Maria—Martyntje—Aug. 15.
Wit: Gerrit A. and Cathalyntje Hoppe.

BOGERT, Stephen and Sophia—Maria—Aug. 15.
Wit: Albert J. and Maria Bogert.

VAN RYPEN, Frederik and Maria—Maria, b. June 6—Aug. 3.
Wit: Harmen and Maria Van Rypen.

POST, John and Annatje—Maria, b. Nov. 13—Dec. 19.
Wit: Richard Davids and Maria Post.

1791

ACKERMAN, Gerrit and Geertje - Maria, b. Jan. 29 - Feb. 24.
Wit: Andries and Maria Hoppe.

SNYDER, Thomas and Maria - Maria, b. Mar. 2 - Apr. 3.

ACKERMAN, Abraham and Elisabeth - Magdalena, b. Apr. 9 - June 22.
Wit: Gerrit G. and Jannetje Ackerman.

DETE, Abraham and Hannah - Maragrietje, b. July 1 - July --.

VAN WEST, Abraham and Esther - Martha, b. Feb 12 - Oct. --.
Wit: Isaak Van Wert and Betsey Schoemaker.

1792

VALENTYN, Wiert and Metje—Margrietje, b. Feb. 6—Feb. —.
Wit: Hendrik Valentyn and Ariaantje Myer.

EARL, John and Rachel—Myntje, b. Mar. 1—Apr. —.
Wit: Gerrit A. and Cathalyntje Hoppe.

SARVENT, Jacob and Annatje—Maria and Catriena (twins)—May 31.
Wit: Lourens and Maria Van Boskerk; Teunis and Catriena Krom.

WOERTENDYK, Jacobus and Sara—Maria, b. May 29—May 31.
Wit: Ryer and Maria Ryerse.

TEYSEN, Hendrik and Maria—Maragrietje, b. May 16—May 31.
Wit: Abraham Teysen.

STAULS, Charles and Jannetje—Margrieta, b. Aug. 9.

BANTA, Jacob and Hester—Margrietje—Oct. 21.

BOGERT, Petrus P. and Margrietje—Maria, b. Jan. 25.
Wit: Petrus and Maria Bogert.

BLAUVELT, Isaak, Jr. and Sara—Maria—Jan. 13.

1789

CHAPPLE, Thomas and Maria—Maria—Jan. 25.
Wit: Abraham and Elisabeth Hopper.

FISHER, Rynder and Polly—Maria, b. Dec. 11, 1788—Feb. 8.
Wit: David and Liesje Fisher.

1793

SHURTE, Adolph and Elisabeth—Margrietje, b. Mar. 3, 1792-Feb. 24.

ACKERMAN, Abraham and Salome—Maria, b. Feb. 16—Mar. 10.
Wit: Jan A. and Maria Hoppe.

KNEGT, Coenraad and Grietje—Martienus, b. Nov. 13, 1792—Mar. 10.

PERRY, Johannis and Dirkje—Maria, b. Dec. 30, 1792—Apr. 14.
Wit: Isaak and Maria Haaring.

MUYSINGER, Coenraad and Catriena—Margrietje—May 19.
Wit: John Muysinger; Margrietje Backer.

DEMAREST, Leah—Margrietje.
Wit: Cornelius and Elisabeth Demarest.

DURIE, Jan and Rachel—Maria, b. Aug. 25—Sep. 22.
Wit: Jacobus and Maria Bogert.

DECKER, William and Aaltje—Margrietje, b. Sep. 16—Oct. 27.

DAYTOR, Adam and Syntje—Maragrietje, b. Oct. 6—Nov. 17.

1794

VRERIKSE, Abraham and Elisabeth—Maragrietje, b. Dec. 7, 1793—Jan. 1.

VALENTYN, Hendrik and Maria—Maria, b. Feb. 11—Mar. 24.
Wit: Felter Swin; Maria Valentyn.

VANDIEN, Dirk and Geertje—Maria—Apr. 20.
Wit: Joost and Maria Bogert.

SCHOERTES, Adolph and Elisabeth—Metje, b. Apr. 16—May 4.
Wit: Pieter and Metje Woertendyk.

HOPPE, Abraham and Geertje—Maria, b. May 31—July 20.

WOERTENDYK, Jan and Elisabeth—Marjeree, b. June 22—July 20.
Wit: Jacobus and Marjeree Anderson.

HORN, Joseph and Ebby—Maria, b. Mar. 31—July 27.

DILL, George and Dortie Gable—Maria, b. July 1—July 27.

VAN WERT, William and Esther—Martha, b. Jan. 3—Aug. 10.
Wit: William Vanwert; Esther Odem.

DEMAREST, Simon and Maria—Maatje, b. Jan. 15, 1791—Aug. 24.

VALENTYN, Wiert and Metje—Maria, b. Aug. 6—Aug. 24.

DECKER, Cornelis and Lea—Margrietje, b. Sep. 10—Sep. 28.

BERBERO, Casparus and Maria—Maragrietje—Nov. 30.
Wit: Matheus and Maragrietje Berbero.

1795

ECKERSON, Nicholas and Maria—Maria, b. Dec. 10, 1794—Feb. 1.
Wit: Jacob and Maria Eckerson.

TERHUNE, Albert and Rachel—Marten, b. Feb. 9—Mar. 8.
Wit: Hendrik and Maria Terhune.

PULISFELT, Pieter and Elisabeth—Maria, b. Mar. 25—Apr. 19.

SHARP, Morris and Elisabeth—Matheus, b. Feb. 22—Apr. 28.

1786

V. BLERKOM, David and Polly—Maria—June 18.
Wit: Jan and Maria Eckerson.

SMITH, Petrus and Jannetje—Maria, b. July 14—Aug. 13.
Wit: Jan and Elisabeth Smith.

OSBORN, James and Maria—Margrietje, b. Sep. 1—Oct. 1.

HOPPE, Hendrik and Aaltje—Marytje, b. Sep. 14—Oct. 1.
Wit: Jan and Maria Zabriske.

DATER, John and Polly—Margrietje, b. Oct. 18—Nov. 12.
Wit: Lodewyk Bush; Margrietje Shulters.

BANTA, Hendrik and Margrieta—Margrietje, b. Oct. 20—Dec. 3.
Wit: Jan and Elisabeth Banta.

1787

FERSYEUR, Abraham and Elisabeth—Magdalena, b. Feb. 3—Mar. 4.
Wit: Johannis and Rebecka Fersyeur.

ALYEE, Samuel and Catriena—Maria—Feb. 11.

WANNEMAKER, Pieter and Hester—Maria—Apr. 9.
Wit: Maria Wannemaker.

TERHUNE, Abraham O. and Sukie—Maria, b. June 27—July 15.
Wit: Thomas and Polly Van Boskerk.

SMYTH, Jacobus and Catriena—Maria, b. July 14—Aug. 1.
Wit: Petrus and Jannetje Smith.

TERHEUN, Hendrik and Rachel—Marytje, b. Aug. 2—Aug. 19.
Wit: Stephen and Geertje Hoppe.

JENKINS, Gerrit and Elisabeth—Margrietje, b. July 28—Aug. 26.

VAN HORN, Daniel and Annatje—Metje, b. Aug. 8—Sep. 9.

BERVOORT, Samuel and Martyntje—Maria, b. Aug. 26—Sep. 27.

FREDERIKS, John and Maria—Maria—Oct. 28.
Wit: Jacob and Maria Conklin.

RYERS, Ryer and Maria—Michael, b. Oct. 20—Nov. 11.

1788

SIDMAN, Samuel and Jannetje—Maria—Jan. 13.
Wit: William and Maria Vos.

DEMAREST, David and Margrietje—Maria—Feb. 3.

VANDERBEEK, Jan and Aaltje—Maria, b. Jan. 19—Feb. 24.
Wit: Jan and Angonietje Westervelt; Abraham and Sara Vanderbeek.

VANBLERKOM, Pieter and Christina—Maritje—Apr. 20.
Wit: Jan and Maritje Vanblerkom.

WATSENS, Pieter and Maragrietje—Maria, b. Oct. 11—Nov. 2.
Wit: Hendrik and Maria Bos.

HOPPER, Abraham and Geertje—Marietje, b. Oct. 26—Nov. 9.
Wit: Jan and Marietje Zabriskie.

PIETERSON, Thomas and Sally—Maria, b. May 23—June 21.
Wit: Nicholaas and Maria Pieterson.

V. D. BEEK, Arie and Lena—Maria, b. June 5—July 12.

DEMAREST, Cornelis and Maria—Margrietje, b. Aug. 19—Oct. 18.

GOETSCHIUS, Nathan and Maria—Matheus, b. July 8—Aug. 16.

ECKERSON, Edward and Hetty—Maria, b. Oct. 8—Nov. 8.
Wit: Laurens and Maria Van Boskerk.

ACKERMAN, Johannis and Sara—Maria, b. Oct. 2—Nov. 1.
Wit: Petrus and Maria Ackerman.

1796

BANTA, Jacob and Hester—Margrietje, b. Jan. 1—Jan 24.

MEBE, Pieter and Jannetje—Maria, b. Jan. 5—Jan. 24.
Wit: Abraham and Maria Mebe.

WESTERVELT, Albert and Maria—Martyntje, b. Jan. 12—Feb. 28.

DEBAAN, Petrus and Maria—Maria, b. Feb. 20—Mar. 20.

CUYPER, Gerrit and Geertje—Margrietje, b. July 26—Aug. 7.

WOERTENDYK, Cornelius and Sophia—Marietje, b. May 15—July 3.

VANBLERKOM, John and Elisabeth—Margrietje, b. Oct. 31—Dec. 25.

1797

DEMAREST, Simon and Cornelia—Maria, b. Jan. 16—Feb. 19.

RIDDENAAR, Coenrad and Elizabeth—Margrietje, b. Nov. 17, 1796—Jan. 2.
Wit: Pieter and Margrietje Watson.

HOPPE, Isaac and Rachel—Martyntje, b. Mar. 18—Apr. 16.
Wit: Gerrit and Cathalyntje Hoppe.

TERHUEN, Abraham and Tryntje—Maria, b. Mar. 31—Apr. 23.

POWEL, John and Klaasje—Maria, b. Apr. 8—June 4.

SNYDER, Thomas and Maria—Margrietje, b. July 8—Aug. 20.

1798

DEBAAN, Andrias and Jannetje—Maria, b. Jan. 4—Feb. 11.

DEMAREST, Simon and Maria—Maria, b. Jan. 20—Feb. 11.

LABACH, Lena—Maretje Yeomans, b. Oct. 2, 1797—Feb. 11.

VAN DIEN, Albert and Maria—Maria, b. Jan. 31—Mar. 4.

DETOR, Adam and Rosina—Matheus, b. Mar. 2—Apr. 1.
Wit: Matheus and Grietje Berbero.

ACKERMAN, Abraham and Sara—Metje, b. Feb. 28—Apr. 15.
Wit: David D. and Sara Ackerman.

BOGERT, Cornelis and Catriena—Maria, b. Apr. 22—May 29.

WOERTENDYK, Reinier and Annaatje—Marlena, b. Apr. 8—June 3.

MESSEKER, Dirk and Leentje—Maria, b. Feb. 24—June 17.

DECKER, Cornelius and Lea—Maria, b. May 23—June 17.
Wit: Johannes and Maria Myer.

1799

ECKERSON, Thomas and Susanna—Maragrietje, b. Dec. 8, 1798—Jan. 6.

DEMAREST, Nikolaas and Maria—Maragrietje, b. Sep. 27, 1798—Jan. 16.

SMITH, Jores and Geertje—Maragrietje, b. June 1—July 17.

STORM, Hendrik and Margrietje—Maria, b. June 24—July 14.
Wit: Coenradus and Maria Storm.

HOPPE, Isaac and Rachel—Maria, b. June 25—July 14.
DOUGHTY, Robert and Mary—Margrieta, b. Mar. 11—Sep. 1.
GUY, John and Sally—Maria, b. Oct. 23—Dec. 15.
VALENTINE, Hendrik and Maria—Margretje, b. Oct. 17—Dec. 22.
Wit: Coenraad and Margrietje Knegt.

1800

ZABRISKIE, Jacob and Elisabeth—Margretha, b. Dec. 29, 1799—Jan. 23.
Wit: Gilliam and Margrietje Terhune.
HOPPER, Andrew and Sara—Margrietje, b. Jan. 26—Mar. 30.
ZABRISKIE, Abraham J. and Susanna—Maria, b. Mar. 17—Apr. 13.
VALENTINE, John and Elisabeth—Margrietje, b. Feb. 6—May 4.
Wit: Coenraad and Margrietje Knegt.
DEBAAN, Albert and Maatje—Margrietje, b. July 1—July 13.
Wit: Joost and Margrietje Debaan.
BLAUVELT, Cornelius and Jannetje—Maria, b. Sep. 2—Sept. 28.
Wit: Abraham and Maria Blauvelt.
HOPPER, Garet and Maria—Maria, b. Nov. 14—Nov. 30.
YEOMENS, John and Trientje—Margrietje, b. Oct. 22—Nov. 30.

1755

HOPPE, Jan A. and Lisabeth—Nicasie, b. May 15—June 15.
Wit: Gerrit H. and Cornelia Kip.

1759

ZABRISKE, Hendrik C. and Maria—Neesje—Jan. 21.
Wit: Hannes and Maritje Vanhoren.
WANNEMAKER, Willem and Catrientje—Niklaas—June 24.
Wit: Coenraad and Marytje Wannemaker.
WESSELS, Joseph and Ariaantje—Niklaas, b. July 7—July 27.
Wit: Benjamin and Nancy Ooldes.

1763

WESSELS, Joseph and Ariaantje—Nellie, b. Oct. 21—Nov. 4.
Wit: Jan and Styntje Ackerman.

1766

ZABRISKIE, Jan and Marytje—Niklaas—Dec. 18.
Wit: Niklaas and Rachel Zabriskie.

1769

ECKERSEN, Jan and Marytje—Niklaas—Sep. 10.
Wit: Niklaas and Matje Volk.

1771

ESSILI, Jan and Lisabeth—Nellie—Oct. 20.
Wit: Isaac and Lena Stagg.

1772

ZABRISKIE, Benjamin and Annatje—Niklaas—May 17.
Wit: Niklaas and Rachel Zabriskie.

1776

STORM, Isaak and Sara—Niklaas—May 5.
Wit: Niklaas and Metje Volk.

1778

NELSON, John and Lisabeth—Nikolaas, b. July 30—Aug. 11.

1781
BROUWER, Jacob and Tryntje—Nikolaas—Nov. 11.
Wit: Albert T. and Mettie Zabriskie.

1786
PIETERSON, Nikolaas and Maria—Nikolaas, b. Oct. 4—Oct. 22.
Wit: Nikolaas and Elisabeth Halderom.

1793
VAN ALEN, Gerrit and Geertje—Neesjen, b. Dec. 9, 1792—May 12.
CERRELLACH, John and Leentje—Nikolaas, b. Sep. 15—Oct. 20.
Wit: Coenraad Backer; Betje Cerrellach.

1795
HOPPE, Gerrit and Maria—Nicasie, b. Jan. 16—Feb. 15.
Wit: Nicasie and Maria Hoppe.

1800
PIETERSON, John and Lise Barbera—Nikolaas, b. Feb. 17—Mar. 19.
Wit: Nicolaas and Maria Pieterson.

1759
DEVENPOORT, Nathaniel and Grietje—Omphre—Jan. 31.
Wit: Omphre & Lisabeth Devenpoort.

1768
MILLER, James and Mary Devenpoort—Omphre—May 25.

1774
SMITH, Abram and Catriena—Omphre, b. Feb. 17—June 28.

1800
VAN VOORHEES, Nicausie and Belitje—Osseltje, b. Dec. 9, 1799(?)—
Jan. 8.
Wit: Dirk & Osseltje Brinkerhoff.

1801
VANDERBEEK, Coenradus and Annatje—Osseltje, b. Nov. 28, 1800(?)—
Mar. 8.

1749
EISTERLI, Marte and Gouda—Pieter—May 2.
Wit: Ryer & Abigael Debouw.

1751
DUBAAN, Jacob and Marytje—Pieter—Mar. 3.
Wit: Andries & Jannitje Dubouw.
ACKERMAN, Albert and Rachel—Pryntje—Jan. 20.
Wit: Frederik & Saartje Cadmus.

1753
ECKER, Thomas and Marytje—Petrus, b. Apr. 26.
Wit: Jacob & Rachel De Marest.
DERYIE,, Daniel and Vrouwtje—Petrus—Oct. 14.
Wit: Jan Deryee.
WANNEMAKER, Hermanus and Susan—Pieter, b. Oct. 1—Oct. 28.
Wit: Pieter & Claartje Wannemaker.

1754
DUBAEN, Jacob and Marytje—Petrus—Mar. 24.
Wit: Samuel & Rebecka Bos.
VAN BLERCOM, Hannes and Marytje—Petrus—Mar. 30.
Wit: Jacobus W. Van Voorhees; Santje A. Rutan.

DEY, Teunis and Esther—Philip, b. July 10—Aug. 4.
Wit: Philip & Anna Schuyler.

ALYEE, Isaac and Annatje—Petrus, b. Sep. 29—Sep. 29.
Wit: Hannes & Annatje Alyee.

1755

VAN BLERKOM, Pieter and Susanna—Petrus—Jan. 26.
Wit: Albert S. & Saartje Terhuyn.

DEBOW, Ryer and Abigael—Pieter—Aug. 3.
Wit: Pieter & Maragriet Debouw.

1756

ACKERMAN, Abram J. and Hester—Petrus, b. May 11—May 30.
Wit: Jan P. & Willempje Demarest.

DEMAREST, Samuel and Lea—Petrus—June 27.
Wit: Pieter D. Demarest.

RIDDENAAR, Hendrik and Grietje—Petrus—June 27.
Wit: Adolf & Lena Myer.

1757

VAN ZEYL, Egbert and Willempje—Pieter—Oct. 22.
Wit: Pieter & Margriet Dubouw.

1758

REP, Johan Cor. and Lisabeth—Petrus—June 25.
Wit: Pieter & Marytje Vonck.

1759

DEMAREST, Petrus S. and Maria—Petrus, b. May 2—May 20.
Wit: Petrus D. & Sara Demarest.

1760

DEY, Teunis and Esther—Petrus, b. Mar. 1—Mar. 30.
Wit: Pieter P. Schuyler and Maria Dey.

ACKERMAN, Niklaes and Maria—Petrus—May 27.
Wit: Petrus S. Dumare and Vrouwtje Westervelt.

1761

DUREMES, Hendrik and Grietje—Pryntje, b. Aug. 4—Aug. 30.
Wit: Thomas Duremes and Geertje Van Winkel.

PECKER, Jacob—Philippus—Dec. 20.
Wit: Philippus Hofman.

1763

VESEUR, Hannes and Lena—Pieter, b. July 12—Aug. 30.
Wit: Pieter & Maria Veseur.

BROUWER, Abram D. and Antje—Petrus—Aug. 30.
Wit: Hendrik & Lena Vanblerkom.

1765

VANHOREN, Dirk B. and Lisabeth—Pieter, b. Apr. 8—Apr. 28.
Wit: Andries & Jannitje Debow.

1766

JONG, Hendrik and Annatje—Phebe—Apr. 6.

1768

PULISFELT, Hendrik and Cornelia—Petrus, b. Oct. 19—Nov. 13.
Wit: Pieter Pilesfelt.

1769

V. DERBEEK, Paulus and Rachel—Paulus—Jan. 29.
Wit: Jacob & Jannitje Brouwer.

BOGERT, Petrus and Maria—Petrus, b. Oct. 22—Nov. 12.
Wit: Petrus & Maria Ackerman.

1771

MAYBE, Jan and Lea—Petrus—Jan 20.
Wit: Pieter Maybe, Jr. & wife.

VAN BLERKOM, Pieter H. and Jannitje—Petrus—Feb. 24.
Wit: Abram & Lisabeth Van Blerkom.

PERRY, Daniel and Jannitje—Pieter & Maria, b. Sep. 24—Oct. 13.
Wit: Pieter & Lisabeth Perry; Pieter & Maria Verseur.

POST, Pieter A. and Geertje—Petrus, b. Nov. 7—Dec. 15.
Wit: Roelof Jacobusse, Grietje Post.

1772

VANBLERKOM, David J. and Gerritje—Petrus—Jan. 26.
Wit: Pieter & Jannitje Maybe.

ECKERSON, David and Angonietje—Paulus—Mar. 15.
Wit: Paulus C. & Annatje Vanderbeek.

1773

ECKERSEN, Thomas T. and Cornelia—Petrus, b. Oct. 9—Nov. 7.
Wit: Petrus & Maria Dubaan.

1774

WESTERVELT, Casparus and Rachel—Petrus, b. Aug. 17—Sep. 4.
Wit: Pieter J. & Annatje Dumaree.

VANBOSKERK, Abram A. and Femmitje—Paulus, b. Mar. 19—Apr. 9.
Wit: Paulus J. & Rachel Vanderbeek.

V. BLERKOM, Johannis and Rebecka—Petrus, b. Jan. 19—Feb. 4.
Wit: Petrus & Antje Van Blerkom.

1776

MESSEKER, Abram and Rachel—Petrus—Mar. 10.
Wit: Petrus & Antje Van Blerkom.

VANBLERKOM, David H. and Polly—Petrus—May 26.
Wit: Petrus P. & Lena H. Van Blerkom.

JERSEY, Pieter and Annatje——Annatje—Aug. 25.
Wit: Hendrik & Geertrui Servent.

1779

ACKERMAN, David A. and Jacomyntje—Pieter—Dec. 12.
Wit: David & Rachel Hoppe.

1780

DE PYSTER, Abraham and Carstina—Peter Rosevelt—Nov. 19.

1779

WESTERVELT, Abraham and Antje—Petrus, b. Aug. 14—Sep. 14.

1781

VAN ZILE, Albert and Rachel—Petrus—Feb. 25.
Wit: Petrus & Jannetje Van Sile.

1782

HENDRIK, Pieter—Pieter—June 25.

1786

POST, Abraham and Jannetje—Petrus, b. Mar. 11—May 21.
VAN SYL, Hermanus and Elisabeth—Polly, b. May 17—June 18.
Wit: Pieter & Susanna Debouw.
TAYLOR, William and Phebe—Phebe, b. Apr. 1—Oct. 1.

1787

VANDER BEEK, Arie and Lena—Paulus, b. Sep. 25—Nov. 11.
Wit: Paulus & Annatje Vanderbeek.

1788

FISBAG, Stephen and Catriena—Petrus, b. Oct. 23—Nov. 9.
Wit: Petrus Muysinger and Sientje Vos.
PERRY, John and Charity—Polly—Nov. 16.
Wit: Hendrik & Peggy Valentyn.

1789

BOVENHUYSEN, Nikolaas and Grietje—Pieter—Jan. 11.
Wit: Hendrik & Sally Poelisfelt.
V. ZEYL, Hermanus and Elisabeth—Pieter, b. Jan. 11—Feb. 1.
Wit: Robert McCall and Betsy Conklin.
DATEY, Abraham and Hannah—Polly, b. Feb. 8—Mar. 22.
Wit: Andrias & Catriena Hopper.
POST, Johannis and Catriena—Pieter—July 5.
Wit: Casparus & Maria Cogh.

1790

DEMAREST, David and Margrietje—Petrus, b. Aug. 22, 1789—Jan. 31.
Wit: Jacob & Annatje Eckerson.
POST, Pieter and Rachel—Petrus—Dec. 19.

1791

BRUYN, Marten and Annatje—Pieter Post, b. Oct. 11, 1790—Jan. 1.
Row, Pieter and Elisabeth—Petrus, b. July 16—Aug. 14.
Wit: Pieter & Maria Pulisvelt.
Bos, Samuel and Lena—Pieter, b. July 30—Sep. 11.
Wit: William & Annaatje Van Voorheesen.
VANDERBEEK, Paulus and Margrietje—Paulus, b. Sep. 21—Nov. 16.

1792

DEBOW, Johannis and Margrietje—Pieter, b. Jan. 16—Feb. 26.
Wit: Pieter & Rachel Vanhorn.
BOSCH, Lodewyk and Lena—Pieter, b. Feb. 25—June 16.
Wit: Dirk & Antje Bosch.
ACKERMAN, Gerrit G. and Jannetje—Petrus, b. Sep. 13—Sep. 16.
Wit: Pieter & Maria Pulisvelt.
DEI, Solomon and Sally—Polly—Sep. 30.

1793

FRERIKSE, Hendrik and Grietje—Pieter, b. Jan. 28—Mar. 10.
WOERTENDYK, Reinier and Annatje—Petrus, b. Jan. 8—Mar. 31.
PULISFELT, Petrus and Nanny—Pieter, b. Feb. 15—Apr. 14.
GERRITSEN, Johannis and Maria—Pieter, b. Oct. 1—Oct. 27.

1793. FRERIKSE, Hendrik and Grietje - Pieter, b. Jan. 28 - Mar. 10.
WOERTENDYK, Reinier and Annatje - Petrus, b. Jan. 8 - Mar. 31.
PULISFELT, Petrus and Nanny - Pieter, b. Feb. 15 - Apr. 14.
GERRITSEN, Johannis and Maria - Pieter, b. Oct. 1 - Oct. 27.

1794. SISCO, Willem and Elisabeth - Polly, b. Dec. 13, 1793 - Jan. 19.
Wit: Richard & Santje De Groot.
BOGERT, Albert J. and Maria - Pieter - Mar. 24.
Wit: Eva Bogert.
BOS, Lodewyk and Leentje - Pieter, b. May 22 - June 29.
Wit: Dirk & Antje Bos.
JOHNSON, Hugh and Rachel - Pieter, b. July 11 - July 27.
BOS, Pieter and Phrone - Pieter, b. July 10.
Wit: Reinhart & Elisabeth Bos.
VAN BLERKOM, Johannis and Elisabeth - Petrus - Aug. 31.
Wit: Petrus & Maria Van Blerkom.
PECKER, Coenraad and Klaartje - Pieter, b. Sep. 3 - Sep. 28.
BROUWER, Jan and Catriena - Pieter, b. Oct. 12 - Nov. 9.
ROW, Philip and Maria - Petrus, b. Sep. 29 - Nov. 23.
Wit: Albert & Rachel Van Zeyl.

1795. VAN ZYL, Hermanus and Elisabeth - Polly, b. Jan. 1 - Mar. 29.
Wit: Thomas & Geertje Myer.
VANHOUTEN, John and Margrietje - Paulus - Apr. 19.
Wit: John & Elisabeth Stagge.
V. ZEYL, Abraham and Rachel - Petrus, b. Nov. 8 - Dec. 13.

1797. WOERTENDYK, Pieter and Metje - Pieter, b. June 15 - July 9.
DEMAREST, Jacob and Geesje - Pieter, b. July 3 - Aug. 20.
Wit: Pieter and Antje Hoppe.
DURIE, Pieter and Osseltje - Pieter, b. Nov. 24 - Dec. 24.

1798. DEMAREST, Albert and Annatje - Pieter, b. Aug. 5 - Aug. 26.
WESTERVELT, Daniel and Elisabeth - Petrus, b. Oct. 27 - Dec. 9.

1799. DEBAAN, Petrus and Ebe - Pieter, b. June 10 - July 7.
DEMAREST, Gileaam and Maatje - Petrus, b. June 9 - Aug. 4.
PERRY, Peter and Margrietje - Peter, b. June 16 - July 13.

1800. DEMAREST, Guileaam and Maatje - Petrus, b. Oct. 12 - Nov. 16.

1750. JURRIKSE, Cobus and Rachel - Rachel - Feb. 17.
Wit: Hannes D. & Rachel Ackerman.
DUBOW, Ryer and Abigael - Rebecka - July 10.
Wit: Samuel & Rebecka Bos.

1751. ZABRISKE, Steven and Tyrntje - Rachel - Mar. 17.
Wit: Albert & Rachel Hoppe.
RYERSE, Marten & Antje - Rachel - June 14.
Wit: Hannes & Rachel Van Rype.

1752. RYER, Jan and Susanna - Ryer - Mar. 8.
Wit: Frederik & Antje Van Rype.
VAN ZEYL, Petrus and Jannitje - Rachel - May 7.
Wit: Hannes A. & Triena Van Zeyl.

1753

HOPPE, Gerrit Jan and Elsje—Rachel—July 29.
Wit: Albert & Rachel Hoppe.

1755

STORM, Abram and Aaltje—Rachel—Nov. 16.
Wit: Hannes & Rachel Storm.

VAN BLERKOM, Lucas and Lisabeth—Ryer—Dec. 26.
Wit: Hannes Ar. & Jakomyntje Ackerman.

1756

HOPPE, Gerrit A. and Hendrika—Rachel, b. May 20—May 30.
Wit: Jacob & Rachel Banta.

1758

HOPPE, Andries and Marytje—Rachel—Jan. 15.
Wit: Steven & Tryntje Zabriske.

1759

KOOL, Hannes and Catriena—Rachel—Jan. 31.
Wit: Jacob & Lea Devenpoort.

WOERTENDYK, Rynier and Jannitje—Rynier—Apr. 9.
Wit: Fredrik & Sara Woertendyk.

HOPPE, Jan J. and Geertje—Rachel—Oct. 21.
Wit: Hendrik J. & Catrintje Hoppe.

1761

HOPPE, Albert and Rachel—Rachel—Mar. 23.
Wit: Pieter & Antje Ackerman.

BOGERT, Lucas and Rachel—Rachel—May 10.
Wit: Pieter A. & Rachel Vanhoute.

DOREMES, Cornelis H.—Rachel, b. Oct. 29—Dec. 6.
Wit: Hendrik & Eegje Deremes.

1762

WOERTENDYK, Frederik and Sara—Reinier, b. May 11—May 30.
Wit: Reinier & Jannitje Woertendyk.

1763

WESTERVELT, Johannes and Antje—Roelof—Oct. 16.
Wit: Roelof & Tryntje Westervelt.

VANDERBEEK, Paulus J. and Rachel—Rachel—Oct. 16.
Wit: Jan & Jannitje Vanderbeek.

1764

VAN GELDER, Jonathan and Marietje—Rachel, b. Apr. 22—May 13.
Wit: Abram & Rachel Van Gelder.

1765

ZABRISKE, Jacob J. and Aaltje—Rachel—Jan. 13.
Wit: Steven & Tryntje Zabriske.

ZABRISKE, Jacob H. and Wyntje—Rachel—July 21.
Wit: Niklaas & Rachel Zabriske.

1766

COCKROW, Niklaas and Pietertje—Rachel—Feb. 9.
Wit: Hendrik & Lena Van Blerkom.

1767

ECKERSON, Jacob and Lea—Rachel—Jan. 4.
Wit: Cornelis & Rachel Eckerson.

ACKERMAN, Albert and Rachel—Rachel—May 3.
Wit: Abram & Marytje Ackerman.

1769

VANBLERKOM, Isaac and Sara—Rachel—Feb. 5.
Wit: Paulus & Rachel Vanderbeek.

1770

TAELMAN, Theunis and Margrietje—Rebecka, b. May 5—May 27 .

ALYEE, Abram and Jacomyntje—Rachel—Dec. 9.
Wit: Albert & Rachel Hoppe.

1771

VANDERBEEK, Abram J. and Santje—Rachel—Jan. 3.
Wit: Hendrik C. & Fytje Banta.

ACKERMAN, David A. and Jacomyntje—Rachel—Mar. 17.
Wit: Gerrit J. & Rachel Ackerman.

STRAAT, Dirk and Rebecka—Rebecka—Apr. 1.
Wit: Jan Straet.

VAN VOORHEESE, Nicasie and Jannitje—Rachel—Apr. 28.
Wit: Albert & Rachel Ackerman.

MYER, Hannes C. and Sara—Rachel—June 30.

BOGERT, Jacob J. and Grietje—Rachel—July 21.
Wit: Jan & Rachel Bogert.

MYER, Cornelis and Ariaantje—Richard—July 21.

1772

ACKERMAN, Petrus and Maria—Rachel—Feb. 16.
Wit: Pieter & Rachel Bogert.

HOPPE, Gerrit H. and Antje—Rachel—Oct. 18.
Wit: Steven & Geesje Bogert.

1773

VAN GELDER, Cobus and Jannitje—Rachel, b. Jan. 18—Jan. 24.
Wit: Jonathan Van Gelder.

VAN BLERKOM, Hannes J. and Rebecka—Ryer—Feb. 21.
Wit: Ryer Debow.

1775

ZABRISKE, Jacob Ja. and Jannitje—Rachel—Jan. 22.
Wit: Jacob & Aaltje Zabriske.

1773

BOGERT, Steven and Geesje—Rachel— Aug. 1.
Wit: Garrit G. & Rachel Gerritse.

VANDERBEEK, Hannes and Abigael—Rachel—Sep. 5.
Wit: Paulus J. & Rachel Vanderbeek.

1774

Bos, Samuel, Jr. and Lena—Rebecka—Feb. 6.
Wit: Samuel & Rebecka Bos.

DOBBS, Willem and Rachel—Rachel—Mar. 20.
Wit: John & Lea Maybe.

1775

VANHOREN, Hannes B. and Rachel—Rachel—Feb. 19.
Wit: Dirk & Lisabeth Vanhoren.

TRAPHAGE, Jonathan and Trientje—Rachel, b. Dec. 11—Dec. 31.

1777

WESTERVELT, Abraham and Antje—Roelof, b. Apr. 12—Apr. 30.
Wit: Johannis & Antje Westervelt.

1780

HOPPE, Jan A. and Marytje—Rachel, b. Nov. 1—Nov. 19.
Wit: Petrus & Rachel Hoppe.

1784

DEBOUW, Pieter—Reinier, b. May 7—June 17.
Wit: Andries Debouw & wife.

GUTSIUS, Piatus—Rachel—May 16.
Wit: ———— & Rachel Westervelt.

1786

LUTKE, Harmen and Antje—Rachel, b. Mar. 1—Mar. 19.
Wit: Hendrik G. & Rachel Hoppe.

HOPPE, Petrus and Elisabeth—Rachel, b. June 27—July 9.
Wit: Abraham & Maria Hoppe.

1787

WOERTENDYK, Cornelis and Sophia—Reinier, b. Aug. 21—Sep. 16.
Wit: Reinier & Jannetje Woertendyk.

1788

BRICKMAN, Lodewyk and Marytje—Reinhart—Jan. 21.
Wit: Pieter & Catriena Swin.

ACKERMAN, John J. and Elsje—Rachel—Jan. 22.

V. D. BEEK, Jacob and Annaatje—Rachel—Aug. 17.
Wit: Paulus & Doortje V. d. Beek.

LABACH, Jan and Maragrietje—Rachel—Nov. 30.

JACOBUSSE, Roelof and Lydia—Rachel—Dec. 7.
Wit: Abraham & Jannetje Vanderbeek.

1789

TAYLOR, Jonas and Ariaantje—Rachel, b. Jan. 21—Mar. 1.

1790

WOERTENDYK, Jacobus and Sara—Rachel, b. Jan. 2—Jan. 24.
Wit: Jan & Rachel Durie.

HOPPER, Gerrit A. and Cathalyntje—Rachel—Jan. 31.
Wit: Isaac & Rachel Hopper.

HOPPE, John and Maria—Rachel—Oct. 17.
Wit: Jacobus & Ariaantje Beem.

1791

WILSON, Albert and Maria—Rachel, b. Aug. 16—Sep. 11.

WOERTENDYK, Albert and Maragrietje—Reinier, b. Sep. 21—Oct. 16.
Wit: Reinier & Jannetje Woertendyk.

1793

VANDERBEEK, Coenradus and Annatje—Rebecka, b. Oct. 2, 1791 (?)—
Feb. 10.
Wit: Samuel & Rebecka Demarest.

HOPPE, Isaac and Rachel—Rachel, b. Mar. 12—Apr. 7.

QUACKENBOS, Leendert and Jannitje—Rensje, b. Mar. 6—Mar. 31.
Wit: Abraham Quackenbos.

ACKERMAN, Johannis and Maria—Rachel, b. Apr. 27—May 19.
Wit: Garrit & Rachel Ackerman.

WOERTENDYK, Jacob—Reinier—Sep. 8.
Wit: Reinier & Jannetje Woertendyk.

WESTERVELT, Roelof and Rachel—Rachel, b. Sep. 15—Oct. 13.

RIDGWAY, John and Peggy—Rachel, b. Sep. 30—Oct. 27.
Wit: Isaac & Catriena Stagg.

1794

VAN VOORHESEN, Abraham and Jannetje Beem—Rachel, b. May 14.

RUTAN, Daniel and Jannitje—Rachel, b. Sep. 7—Sep. 28.
 Wit: Hendrik & Rachel Swin.

BANTA, Abram and Catriena—Rachel, b. July 21—Nov. 2.
 Wit: Jacob & Rachel Banta.

HOPPE, Abraham and Elisabeth—Rachel, b. Oct. 12—Nov. 9.
 Wit: Isaac & Rachel Hoppe.

DEMAREST, Symon and Cornelia—Rebecka, b. Nov. 13—Nov. 30.
 Wit: Joost & Polly Van Boskerk.

1795

BOGERT, Jan and Margrietje—Rachel, b. Feb. 23—Mar. 15.
 Wit: Steven & Maria Bogert.

TYSEN, Pieter and Maria—Rachel, b. Feb. 21—Apr. 19.

MEKRAAF, Martin and Christina—Rachel, b. Nov. 3, 1794—Aug. 23.

1796

WRIGHT, John and Abigael—Rachel, b. July 11—Aug. 7.

DEMAREST, Symon and Maria—Rachel, b. Nov. 23—Dec. 25.

1797

DEMAREST, Albert and Annatje—Rachel, b. Dec. 25, 1796—Jan. 22.
 Wit: John & Rachel Durie.

CERELLACH, George and Jannitje—Robert, b. Sep. 20, 1796—Apr. 17.

BERBERO, Casparus and Maria—Rachel, b. Mar. 20—Apr. 17.
 Wit: John & Rachel Hicks.

ECKERSON, Edward and Catriena—Rachel and Sarah (twins), b. Oct.
 4—Nov. 26.
 Wit: Jacob, Catriena, Petrus & Maria Eckerson.

1800

ANDERSON, Jacobus and Margary—Rebecka, b. Sep. 14, 1799—Apr. 14.

DEMAREST, Symon and Maria—Rachel, b. May 9—July 13.
 Wit: Corynus & Rachel Remsen.

WOERTENDYK, Rynier and Annatje—Rachel, b. Aug. 16—Sep. 7.

1748
STORM, Hendrik and Cornelia—Staats—Nov. 13.
    Wit: Staats & Susannah Storm.

1749
VAN WINKEL, Hannes S. and Janneke—Simeon and Janneke (twins)—
    Dec. 24.
    Wit: Jacob, Vrouwtje, & Jannike Van Winkel; Dirk Ryerse.

1752
VAN WINKEL, Jacob and Vrouwtje—Simeon—Apr. 19.
    Wit: Albert & Rachel Ackerman.

1755
RYER, John and Sunna—Sara—Jan. 12.
    Wit: Frederik & Sara Woertendyk.

DERYIE, Jan D. and Jannitje—Samuel—Nov. 16.
    Wit: Cornelis & Maria Smit.

STORM, Hendrik and Cornelia—Staats—Dec. 14.
    Wit: Staats & Susanna Storm.

1756
OOLDES, Benjamin and Nellie—Sara—May 9.
    Wit: Josie & Ariaantje Wessels.

GALLEWE, John and Lea—Isaak—June —.
    Wit: Steven & Marritje Slot.

VAN RYPE, Fredrik and Saartje—Simeon, b. July 18—Aug. 15.
    Wit: Albert & Rachel Ackerman.

1757
ACKERMAN, Hannes A. and Jakomyntje—Sara—Sep. 4.
    Wit: David A. & Sara Ackerman.

WALDEROM, Hannes and Wyntje—Samme Bense, b. Aug. 28—Sep. 4.
    Wit: Samme Bense and Lisabeth Lydecker.

1758
HOPPE, Gerrit A. and Hendrikje—Steven—Oct. 22.
    Wit: David & Sara Terhuyn.

1759
DEY, Dirk and Sara—Sara—June 24.
    Wit: Jacob & Vrouwtje Van Winkel.

1760
BOS, Samuel and Rebecka—Saartje—June 8.
    Wit: David D. & Saartje Ackerman.

1761
VAN BLERKOM, Gerrit and Hillegont—Samuel—Feb. 22.
    Wit: Lourens Ackerman; Jannetje V (an) Blerkom.

WESSELLS, Joseph and Ariaantje—Sara—July 5.
    Wit: Albert & Rachel Ackerman.

1762

RYER, John and Soike—Susannah—Feb. 14.
   Wit: Isaak & Lisabeth Post.

HELM, Samuel and Catrientje—Samuel, b. Mar. 1—Mar. 20.

1763

BOGERT, Jacob and Marytje—Steven—July 24.
   Wit: Steve & Tryntje Zabriske.

STORM, Hendrik and Cornelia—Susannah—Oct. 2.
   Wit: Abram & Saartje V. derbeek.

1764

WOERTENDYK, Fredrik and Macere—Sara, b. June 5—June 24.
   Wit: Jan P. & Jannitje Deryie.

1765

POST, Isaac and Jannetje—Sara—Nov. 10.
   Wit: Abram & Sara Post.

1766

WOERTENDYK, Frederik and Majeri—Susannah, b. Aug. 8—Aug. 31.
   Wit: John & Susannah Ryer.

1767

ALYEE, Jacobus and Annatje—Saphira (?) Saffya or Saffyee (?)—Jan.
   25.

EKKERSON, Jan and Maria—Susanna—Apr. 12.
   Wit: Jacob & Maria Ekkerson.

1768

FISHER, Joost—Saartje—Mar. 6.

HOPPE, Andries A. and Lisabeth—Saartje, b. Apr. 7—May 5.
   Wit: Abram & Saartje Post.

ZABRISKIE, Hendrik C. and Maria—Sara—June 26.
   Wit: David & Sara Terhune.

LUTKINS, Harme H. and Antje—Steven—Oct. 23.
   Wit: Christiaan A. & Rachel Zabriskie.

1769

ACKERMAN, David (H.?) and Myntje—Sara—Mar. 19.
   Wit: Abram W. & Grietje Rutan.

1770

TOIRS, Lourens and Elisabeth—Sara—Nov. 4.
   Wit: Fredrik & Saartje Cadmus.

1771

POST, Hannes A. and Trientje—Susannah—Apr. 21.
   Wit: Guliaam & Susannah Dumaree.

1772

POST, Abram, Jr. and Jannitje—Saartje—Dec. 6.
   Wit: Abram & Saartje Post.

1773

KOGH, Casper and Lidia—Steven, b. June 3—June 6.
   Wit: Jan J. & Lea Zabriske.

1774

DEVENPOORT, Leendert and Mary—Sara, b. Feb. 7, 1773—June 28.
ACKERMAN, Cornelis and Elisabeth—Lawrence—Aug. 28.
  Wit: David J. & Antje Ackerman.
Bos, Pieter and Annatje—Samuel—Sep. 17.
  Wit: Samuel S. & Lena Bos.

1754

VOLK, Nikolaas and Metje—Sara—Sep. 8.
  Wit: B. & Nellie Odel.
  (Is also to be found under the letter C.)

1775

WOERTENDYK, Frederik and Sara—Jan. 29.
  Wit: Frederik & Majeri Woertendyk.
RUTAN, Johannis A. and Elisabeth—Saartje, b. Sep. 25—Dec. 14.
  Wit: Jacobus & Willempje Rutan.

1776

BENSEN, Matheus and Marytje—Samuel—Jan. 28.
VESEUR, Hannes and Lena—Samuel, b. Jan. 29—Mar. 31.
  Wit: Samuel & Lisabeth Banta.
ZABRISKE, Albert J. and Geesje—Steven—Mar. 31.
  Wit: Steven Zabriskie.
QUACKINBOS, Pieter and Grietje—Susannah, b. June 15—July 7.
  Wit: Willem & Santje Pieterse.

1779

MOUNT, Richard and Rachel—Susannah—Dec. 12.

1781

TERHUYN, Steven and Jannitje—Steven, b. Aug. 28—Oct. 7.
  Wit: Christiaan & Martyntje Zobriske.

1782

BOES, Sam—Sam—Sep. 17.
STORM, Coenradus— ? —Dec. 2.
  Wit: Jacob Eckerse & wife.

1784

HOPPER, Jacob—Sara—Apr. 11.
POST, Abraham—Sannie—Apr. 11.
GEERITSE, Johannis—Sara—Sep. 5.

1785

HOPPE, Jan and Maria—Sally, b. June 5—Sep. 5.
  Wit: Sallie Cuyper.
RYER, Jan and Maria—Sukee—Sep. 25.
  Wit: Sukie Demarest.

1786

ACKERMAN, Johannis and Annaatje—Sara, b. June 6—June 18.
  Wit: Gerrit & Elisabeth Ackerman.
Bos, Jacobus and Aaltje—Samuel, b. May 16—July 2.
  Wit: Samuel & Lena Bos.
BEMPER, Jacob and Antje—Sara Brower—July 17.

Bos, Samuel and Lena—Sara, b. July 18—Aug. —.
Wit: John & Sara Beem.
Tyson, John and Annatje—Saartje, b. Sep. 3—Oct. 1.
Wit: Harmen & Trientje Retan.

1787

Valentyn, Wiert and Metje—Sara, b. May 28—June 17.
Wit: Cornelis & Ariaantje Myer.
Van Dien, Andreas and Sara—Sara—Sep. 9.
Dee, Isaac and Francyntje—Susannah—Sep. 16.
Terhuun, Stephen and Jannetje—Sara—Sep. 30.
Wit: Pieter & Antje Demarest.
Straat, Jan and Sukie—Sukie, b. Oct. 24—Nov. 11.
Banta, Samuel and Elisabeth—Samuel, b. Nov. 26—Dec. 9.
Wit: Abraham & Dievertje Banta.
Eckerson, Edward and Catriena—Susannah, b. Dec. 15—Dec. 30.

1788

Post, Jan J. and Annatje—Sara, b. Mar. 4—Apr. 20.
Wit: Jan & Nancy Post.
Jacobusse, Roelof and Lydia—Susannah and Sara—Dec. 7.
Wit: Abraham & Jannetje Vanderbeek.
Westervelt, Jan and Angonietje—Sara, b. June 6—July 5.
Vandien, Albert and Maria—Sara, b. Aug. 9—Aug. 30.
Wit: Harman & Aaltje Vandien.
Hoppe, Andrias and Catriena—Stephen, b. May 21—Aug. 30.
Wit: Stephen & Geertje Hoppe.

1790

Banta, Hendrik and Maria—Sietsje, b. Aug. 11—Aug. 15.
Wit: Cornelis & Sietsje Bogert.
Eckerson, Thomas and Susannah—Sara, b. Apr. 4—May 2.
Wit: Jacobus & Sara Demarest.

1791

Debow, Petrus and Susannah—Sara, b. Dec. 27, 1790—Jan. 30.
Terhune, John and Catriena—Steven, b. Feb. 1—Feb. 24.
Wit: Steven Lutken and Lea Blauvelt.
Durjee, Jan and Rachel—Sara, b. Apr. 2—Apr. 25.
Wit: Jacobus & Sara Woertendyk.
Perry, John and Charity—Sally, b. Mar. 26—Apr. 25.
Benner, Jeams and Geesje—Samuel, b. Apr. 17—May 29.
Rotan, Jan and Rachel—Sara, b. Sep. 10—Oct. 9.
Wit: Abraham & Maria Rotan.
Post, Johannis and Catriena—Samuel b, Aug. 22—Oct. 9.
Wit: Jacob & Maria Kogh.

1792

Van Zeyl, Hermanus and Elisabeth—Susannah—Feb. 26.
Wit: Pieter & Susannah Debow.
Vanhorn, David and Sara—Sara—Nov. 11.

1794

RATAN, John and Rachel—Susannah, b. Nov. 28, 1793 (?)—Jan. 2.
Wit: Abraham & Susannah V. d. Beek.

RATAN, Abraham and Maria—Sara, b. Apr. 20—May 4.
Wit: Jacobus & Willempje Ratan.

DEBOUW, John and Margrietje Aljee—Syntje, b. Apr. 4—May 4.

BERTOLF, Jacobus and Metje Post—Sally, b. Dec. 24—May 4.

ZABRISKE, Albert and Metje—Simeon, b. Sep. 20—Oct. 26.

STORM, Isaac and Elisabeth—Saartje, b. July 29—Oct. 1.

1795

McCALL, Alexander and Rachel—Sara, b. Nov. 23, 1794—Feb. 1.
Wit: John & Sara Van Blerkom.

POST, Pieter and Rachel—Sara, b. June 10—June 28.

MYER, Thomas and Geertje—Sara, b. Sep. 21—Oct. 18.

1796

DURIE, Samuel and Catriena—Sara, b. Dec. 13, 1795—Jan. 1.
Wit: Thomas & Sara Pieterson.

SISCO, Willem and Elisabeth—Semme, b. Dec. 7, 1795—Jan. 24.

1797

DEBAAN, Jacob and Osseltje—Samuel, b. Jan. 25—Feb. 19.
Wit: Samuel & Rebecka Demarest.

TERHUNE, John S. and Antje—Stephen, b. May 4—May 21.

POTTER, John and Maria—Samuel, b. June 20—July 3.

TERHUNE, Jan and Eva—Sara, b. June 27—Aug. 20.
Wit: Christiaan & Maria Zabriskie.

REYER, Reyer and Maria—Soecke, b. Sep. 5—Oct. 1.

VANDERBEEK, Arie and Lena—Sara, b. Oct. 18—Nov. 26.

1798

REYER, John and Maria—Syntje, b. Apr. 27—June 3.
Wit: Barend & Francyntje Fesyeur.

STORM, Staats and Maragrietje—Susannah, b. May 15—June 3.

DEMAREST, David and Geesje—Samuel, b. Apr. 8—Oct. 14.
Wit: Samuel & Rebecka Demarest.

1799

BERDAN, John I. and Mary—Stephen, b. Nov. 28—Dec. 20.

1800

DEMAREST, Albert and Annatje—Samuel, b. Oct. 1—Oct. 26.
Wit: Samuel & Catriena Durie.

1750

BOGERT, Lucas and Doritie—Tryntje—Nov. 11.
Wit: Steven & Tryntje Zabriskie.

1752

HOPPE, Hendrik and Trientje—Trientje—Apr. 19.
Wit: Albert & Rachel Hoppe.

1755

IESTERLI, Marte and Gouda—Thomas—Dec. 14.
Wit: Benjamin & Neeltje Oldes.

1756

ECKENSEN, Jacob and Susannah Maria—Thomas, b. May 3—May 30.
Wit: Thomas & Maria Eckesen.
TOIRS, Lourens and Lisabeth—Thomas—Aug. 8.
Wit: Dirk & Saartje Dey.

1760

ECKESEN, Jan and Lena—Thomas, b. May 26—June 14.
Wit: Thomas & Maria Eckesen.

1761

BERTOLF, Hannes and Wybrecht—Trientje—June 14.
Wit: Willem & Antje Hoppe.

1762

MYER, Hannes C. and Sara—Thomas, b. Mar. 13—Apr. 13.
Wit: Thomas & Maria Eckersen.
ECKERSEN, David and Angonietje—Thomas, b. June 27—July 18.
Wit: Thomas & Marytje Eckersen.
ECKERSEN, David and Angonietje—Thomas—Sep. 5, 1762 (?).
Wit: Thomas & Marytje Eckerson.
TOERS, Lourens and Lisabeth—Thomas—Oct. 17.
Wit: Dirk D. Dey & wife.

1764

VAN ORDER, Andries and Lisabeth—Tryntje—Feb. 5.
Wit: Samuel & Trientje Helm.
BOGERT, Cobus and Cornelia—Tryntje—Apr. 23.
Wit: Roelof & Tryntje Westervelt.

1766

ECKERSON, Jacob T. and Jannetje—Thomas, b. Aug. 14—Aug. 31.
Wit: Thomas & Maria Eckersen.

1767

BONGAERT, Steven and Rachel—Trientje—Feb. 15.
Wit: Gerrit H. & Antje Hoppe.

1768

RIDDENAER, Hendrik and Grietje—Tryntje—Jan. 3.
Wit: Hendrik & Marytje Oldes.
RUTAN, Daniel and Santje—Tryntje—Mar. 27.
Wit: Johannis A. & Trientje Post.
DEY, Teunis and Hester—Teunis, b. Aug. 19—Sep. 18.
Wit: Ariaantje V. de Linde.

1767

MILLIDGE, Thomas and Sarah—Thomas—Nov. 28.

1770

WESTERVELT, Casparus and Wyntje—Trientje—Jan. 14.
VAN GIESE, Isaac R. and Pryntje—Thomas—Jan. 20.
COGH, Casper and Lidea—Trientje—Sep. 30.
Wit: Jacob J. & Jannitje Zabriskie.
GERRITSE, Pieter H. and Effie—Trientje—Aug. 4.
Wit: Hans & Trientje Demodt.

1771

VAN IMBURGH, John and Antie—Tryntje—Nov. 24.
Wit: Cobus J. & Cornelia Bogert.

1772

STEGG, Isaac and Lena—Thomas, b. Dec. 13, 1771—Jan. 5.
Wit: Abram & Marytje Ackerman.
BANTA, Samuel and Elisabeth—Thomas, b. Aug. 27.
Wit: Thomas & Maria Eckersen.

1773

VANDIEN, Thomas and Polly—Trientje—Nov. 28.
Wit: Daniel & Vrouwtje Duryie.
PIETERSE, Niklaas—Thomas, b. Jan. 11—Nov. 28.
Wit: Barend & Syntje Veseur.

1775

ECKERSON, Thomas T. and Cornelia—Thomas, b. Apr. 1—May 14.
Wit: Jacob & Jannitje Eckerson.
DOBS, William and Rachel—Trientje, b. Sep. 6—Oct. 22.
Wit: Andries & Trientje Holderom.

1776

POST, Abram and Jannetje—Trientje, b. Feb. 15—Mar. 31.
Wit: Jacob & Saartje Post.

1779

OLDES, Hendrik and Marytje—Tryntje—Apr. 5.
Wit: Roelof Westervelt; Cornelia Bogert.
DEPYSTER, Abraham and Styntje—Steven Baldwin—Apr. 11.
Wit: Antje Baldwin.

1780

VAN BLERKOM, David and Polly—Trientje—Sep. 17.

1781

WESTERVELT, Abraham and Antje—Trientje, b. Aug. 8—Sep. 16.
Wit: Jacobus Bogert and daughter Trientje.
ECKERSON, Edward and Catriena—Thomas, b. Mar. 14—Apr. 9.
Wit: Thomas & Cornelia Eckerson.
TAYLOR, Stephen and Elisabeth—Teunis, b. May 4—Oct. 1.

1788

BERTOLF, Hendrik and Margrietje—Tryntje—Feb. 3.
WESTERVELT, Albert and Margrietje—Tryntje—May 4.
Wit: Jacobus & Cornelia Bogert.
FRERIKSE, Hendrik and Maria—Tryntje—Sep. 28.
BENNER, James and Geesje—Thomas, b. Sep. 12—Oct. 19.
Wit: John & Martina Eckerson.
ROTAN, Jan and Jannetje—Tryntje, b. Nov. 13—Oct. 19.
Wit: Gerrit & Tryntje Blauvelt.

1789

BANTA, Hendrik and Margrietje—Teunis, b. Mar. 25—May 10.
Wit: Teunis & Sara Demarest.

1791

HOPPE, Isaac and Rachel—Teunis, b. Jan. 6—Feb. 6.
Wit: Teunis & Margrietje Cuyper.

1792

STAGGE, John and Elisabeth—Thomas, b. Oct. 8—Nov. 11.
Wit: Thomas & Esther Stagge.

1793

DEBAAN, Jan and Wyntje—Tryntje, b. Sep. 16—Sep. 29.
Wit: Jan. T. Banta.

1794

VAN BOSKERK, Pieter and Sally—Thomas—Mar. 30.
PAULUSSE, John and Klaasje—Teunis, b. Apr. 15—May —.

1795

JANSEN, Abraham and Elisabeth—Tietje, b. Dec. 10, 1794—Jan. 4.
Wit: Jacobus & Tietje Poelisvelt.
BANTA, John and Cornelia—Tryntje, b. Oct. 21—Nov. 8.
Wit: John & Wyntje Debaen.
WILLS, Thomas and Rachel—Thomas, b. Oct. 28—Nov. 15.
Wit: David Marines; Dirkje Ackerman.

1796

BLAUVELT, Joseph and Maria—Trientje, b. Feb. 14—Mar. 27.

1797

GARDNER, Thomas and Aaltje—Thomas, b. Jan. 10—Feb. 19.
VAN AULEN, John and Angonietje—Trientje, b. Feb. 22—Mar. 19.
HOPPER, Gerrit and Maria—Trientje—Sep. 3.
Wit: Jacobus & Trientje Clerck.

1798
BOGERT, Jan and Margrietje—Trientje,. b. Nov. 19—Dec. 9.

1799
MEBE, Abraham and Maria—Trientje, b. Nov. 11, 1798—Jan. 6.

ACKERMAN, Abraham and Maragrietje—Trientje, b. Mar. 15—Apr. 14.
Wit: Petrus & Trientje Ackerman.

CAMPBELL, William and Jannetje—Tietje, b. July 14—July 28.
Wit: John & Tietje Campbell.

1800
VANDIEN, Casparus and Polly—Thomas, b. Dec. 29, 1799—Mar. 2.
Wit: Dirk & Antje Vandien.

ECKERSON, Peter and Margrietje—Thomas, b. Aug. 20—Sep. 7.
Wit: Thomas & Cornelia Eckerson.

VANDERBEEK, Paulus and Margrietje—Tyne, b. Sep. 3—Sep. 21.

SORLIE, Lourens and Elisabeth—Trientje, b. Sep. 16—Nov. 30.
Wit: John & Trientje Terhune.

1763
DUMARE, Petrus S. and Feytje—Vroutje—Oct. 16.
Wit: David S. & Jennie Dumare.

1771
GERRITSE, Gerrebrand and Leentje—Vroutje—Jan. 1.
Wit: Jacob & Vroutje Van Winkel.

1782
VAN RYPE, Gerrit—Vredrik, b. Mar. 8—Apr. 7.
Wit: Harme Van Rype, Jr. & wife.

1793
DEMAREST, Daniel and Maria—Vroutje, b. July 1—Oct. 20.

1795
DEMAREST, Symen and Maria—Vroutje, b. Dec. 10, 1794 (?)—Jan. 11.
Wit: Frederik & Vroutje Woertendyk.

"W"

1751
BOGERT, Cornelis J. and Lena—Willemtie—Jan. 1.
Wit: Albert & Mechtel Bogerd.

MORE, Jeremiah and Lisabeth—Wilms—Apr. 7.
Wit: Hannes & Marytje Van Blerkom.

1753
VAN VOORHEES, Jan and Lea—Willem—Dec. 30.
Wit: Hannes & Marytje Van Blerkom.

1756
VAN SCHYVEN, Hannes and Vroutje—Willem—May 9.
Wit: Albert & Rachel Ackerman.

1757
BANTA, Jacob W. and Lena—Wiert—Aug. 4.
Wit: Wiert & Geertrui Banta.

1758
SYOURT, Willem and Trientje—Willem—Oct. 22.
Wit: Arie & Lisabeth Laroi.

1759
ZABRISKE, Jacob J. and Aaltje—Wyntje—June 10.
Wit: Jacob H. & Wyntje Zabriske.

1761
MILLS, Thomas and Maaike—Willem—Mar. 29.
Wit: Jurry & Marietje Westervelt.

1762
LANE, Henry and Betsie—Willem Henry—Aug. 1.
Wit: Gerrit & Elsje Hoppe.

1765
TERHUYN, Dirk and Lea—Wyntje—Nov. 10.
. Wit: Jacob H. & Wyntje Zabriskie.

1766
BONGAERT, Lucas and Rachel—Willempje—Mar. 2.
Wit: Cobus & Willempje Rutan.

1767
ZABRISKE, Jacob H. and Wyntje—Wyntje—Mar. 22.
Wit: Hendrik & Wyntje Hoppe.
BOGGS, Thomas and Trientje—Willem—Dec. 23.

1768
TERHUYN, Abram A. and Marytje—Wyntje—Mar. 6.
Wit: Albert A. & Betje Terhuyn.
ZABRISKE, Jacob H. and Wyntje—Wyntje—Nov. 6.
Wit: Hendrik & Wyntje Hoppe.

1789
DOBBS, William and Rachel—Walterus—May 15.
Wit: Abram W. & Grietje Rutan.

1770
HOPPE, Jan W. and Annatje—Willem, b. Jan. 26—Apr. 15.
Wit: Willem & Antje Hoppe.

1771
BOGERT, Cornelis A. and Sietsje—Willempje—Aug. 4.
Wit: Albert R. & Willempje Romyne.

1772
HOMS, Jan, Jr. and Debra—Wyntje—June 28.
Wit: Wyntje Homs.

1773
VERSIEUR, Hannes and Lena—Willem, b. Feb. 15—Mar. 21.
Wit: Willem & Lisabeth Versieur.
VAN BLARCOM, Isaac and Sara—Willem—May 16.
Wit: Douglas & Geesje Carns.
ACKERMAN, Abram and Marytje—Wyntje—Sep. 23.
Wit: Jan J. & Aaltje Hoppe.
LAROI, Hannes and Grietje—Willem—Oct. 10.
Wit: Willem & Margriet Jenkins.

1774

CLEA, Christiaan and Maria—Wilhelm, b. Dec. 4, 1773—June 28.
HOPPE, Abram H. and Antje—Wyntje—July 10.
  Wit: Abram & Marytje Ackerman.

1778

HOPPE, Abram H. and Antje—Wyntje—Nov. 1.
  Wit: Abram & Marytje Ackerman.

1781

BERTOLF, Crynus and Susanna—Wybrecht, b. May 16—June 3.
  Wit: Samuel & Trientje Bertolf.
SHURTE, Isaak and Margriet—Willem—Apr. 7.
  Wit: Albert & Trientje Zabriske.

1782

DE PEYSTER, Abram—Willem Abram—Sep. 5.

1785

ACKERMAN, Abram G.—Willem—Apr. 10.
  Wit: Jacobus Ackerman; Lea Dods.
VANHORN, Jacobus and Lea—William, b. Aug. 1—Oct. 2.

1786

TANNING, or TANNARY, Pieter—William—Feb. 26.
DEE, Salomon and Sally—William, b. Aug. 14—Oct. 1.
  Wit: John & Maria More.

1787

BELL, William and Rachel—William Swan, b. Dec. 27, 1786—Jan. 28.
VALENTYN, Jacob and Elisabeth—William, b. Dec. 26.
  Wit: Wiert & Metje Valentyn.
HARING, Cornelis A. and Antje—Willem, b. Feb. 27—Mar. 25.
HOPPE, Gerrit W. and Margrietje—William, b. Nov. 15—Dec. 25.
  Wit: Andreas W. & Maria Hoppe.

1788

POST, Frederik and Annatje—Wyntje, b. Sep. 5—Dec. 21.
  Wit: John & Wyntje Fesyeur.

1789

V. D. BEEK, Johannis and Abigail—Wyntje, b. Feb. 14—Mar. 8.
  Wit: Thomas & Maria Van Boskerk.
HOPPE, Hendrik and Aaltje—Wyntje, b. Mar. 16—Apr. 4.
  Wit: Johannis & Abigail Vanderbeek.

1790

CAIRNS, David and Elisabeth—William—Mar. 14.

1791

ZABRISKA, Hendrik and Maria—Wyntje—Sep. 29.
  Wit: Jan & Elisabeth Zabriska.

1792

PULISFELT, Coenraad and Elisabeth—William, b. Oct. 3—Nov. 11.
  Wit: Abraham & Catriena Pulisfelt.

1793

POST, Pieter and Rachel—Wyntje, b. Dec. 4, 1792—Feb. 10.
ROUW, Phillip and Maria—William, b. Feb. 22—Mar. 10.
BOSCH, Samuel and Lena—Wybrech, b. July 30—Aug. 18.
  Wit: Thomas & Esther Stagg.
FESYEUR, Cornelius and Jannetje—William, b. Aug. 11—Sep. 8.
  Wit: David & Polly Fesyeur.

1794

VALENTYN, David and Rachel—William, b. Mar. 3—Apr. 20.
Wit: William Eckhart and Maria Valentyn.

VAN ZYL, Abraham and Rachel—William, b. Mar. 30—Apr. 20.
Wit: Johannis Van Zyl and Syntje Ackerman.

WINTER, Lewis and Lena—William, b. June 23—Sep. 14.

GOETSCHIUS, Piatus and Catriena—William, b. Sep. 21—Oct. 19.
Wit: Garret & Geertje Ackerman.

FESYEUR, David and Maria—William, b. Nov. 3—Nov. 16.

1795

WINTER, John and Hendrikje—William, b. Apr. 30—June 14.
Wit: Cornelis & Hattie Degrauw.

FRERIKSE, Hendrik and Margrietje—William, b. Aug. 20—Oct. 18.
Wit: William & Sally Pecker.

1797

DEREST, Lieshon and Elisabeth—Willem and Christina (twins), b. Mar. 24—Apr. 17.
Wit: Salomon & Sally Dee.

FERGUSON, Samuel and Jannetje—William, b. Aug. 16—Nov. 26.

1798

CUYPER, Geerit and Geertrui—Willemyntje, b. Oct. 27—Dec. 9.

ROTAN, Abraham and Lydia—Willempje, b. Nov. 8—Dec. 9.
Wit: Willempje Rotan.

1800

ECKERSON, Cornelius and Catriena—William, b. May 7, 1799—Mar. 30.

WRIGHT, Albert and Annatje—William, b. Apr. 16—May 18.

LIST OF MEMBERS, 1799

List of Members found by Rev. Wilhelmus Eltiinge, at the time of his family-visitation through the Congregation of Paramus about May 1, 1799.

JACOB ZABRISKIE and wife Jannetje.
HARMEN LUTKENS and wife Antje.
ALBERT ZABRISKIE and wife Metje.
ANTJE ZABRISKIE, widow of Jacob.
WYNTJE ZABRISKIE.
GARRET HOPPER.
JOHN I. ZABRISKIE and wife Leah.
JOST BOGERT and wife Maria.
CHRISTIAN ZABRISKIE and wife Maria.
ANDRIES ZABRISKIE and wife Maria.
CHRISTIAN A. ZABRISKIE and wife Maria.
JOHANNIS H. GARRISON and wife Maria.
CASPARIS BOGERT and wife Jannitje.
MARIA ZABRISKIE, widow of Hendrick.
JANNITJE NAGEL, widow of Barend.
JACOB ZABRISKIE and wife Helena.
LIDEA KOGH, wife of Casparus.
SUSANNA VAN BERCUM, widow of Peter.
JANNETJE THERHUNE, widow of Stephen.
WYNTJE ZABRISKIE, widow of Jacob H.
ALBERT I. ZABRISKIE and wife Maria.
ABRAHAM ZABRISKIE and wife Maria.
HENDRICK ZABRISKIE.
ABRAHAM WESTERVELT and wife Antje.
JOHANNIS WESTERVELT and wife Annatje.
GARRET ACKERMAN and wife Rachel.
ELSHE HOPPER, widow of Garret.
SAMUEL BANTA and wife, Elisabeth.
PETRUS DEMAREEST and wife, Maatje.
ABRAHAM HOPPER and wife Antje.
GARRET I. HOPPER and wife Maria.
MARIA TERHUNE, wife of Abraham.
STEPHEN BOGERT and wife, Maria.
ABRAHAM RUTAN and Margrietje.
ALBERT A. TERHUNE and wife, Aaltje.
HENRY A. TERHUNE and wife, Rachel.

DAVID G. ACKERMAN and wife Aaltje.
CORNELIUS VAN DIEN.
HILLEGOND VAN DER BEEK.
JOHANNIS VAN DER BEEK and wife Abigail.
PETER HOPPER and wife Annatje.
JOHN R. BERDAN and wife Hendrickie.
JACOMYNTJE ACKERMAN, widow of David.
ABRAHAM QUACKENBUSH.
THEODORUS POLHEMUS and wife Elisabeth.
JACOBUS B. DEMAREST and wife Jannitje.
HENDRICK STORM and wife Cornelia.
CASPARUS WESTERVELT and wife Rachel.
CORNELIUS DEMAREST and wife Maria.
LAWRANCE TOERS and wife Elisabeth.
MARIA VAN DER BEEK, widow of Jusia (or Juria).
ANNATJE VAN DER BEEK, widow of Paulus.
JACOBUS BOGERT and wife Cornelia.
JOHN PULISFELT and wife Elisabeth.
ANTIE ACKERMAN, wife of Albert I.
BENJAMIN ZABRISKIE and wife Annatje.
DANIEL WESTERVELT and wife Elisabeth.

JACOB BANTA and wife Hester.
JOHN BANTA and wife Vrouwtje.
JOHN ZABRISKIE and wife Jacomyntje.
HENDRICK BANTA.
CHRISTIAN BLAUVELT and wife Cathalyntje.
EDWARD ECKERSON and wife Caty.
WILLEMPIE RUTAN, widow of Jacobus.
HENDRICK H. STORM and wife Aaltje.
JOHANNES G. ACKERMAN and wife Elisabeth.
GARRIT VAN RYPER and wife Abigail.

CORNELIUS WORTENDIKE and wife Sophia.
RYNA (?) WORTENDIKE.
BAREND FERSHUIR and wife Francintje.
CATHARINA FERSHUIR, wife of ————.
NICHOLAS HULDROM and wife Helena.
NICHOLAS PETERSON and wife Maria.
ANDRIES HOPPER and wife Elisabeth.
HENDRICK HOPPER and wife Aaltje.
ABRAHAM I. HOPPER and Geertie.
ELISA'TH HOPPER, widow of John.
NICAUSIE HOPPER and wife Maria.
STEPHEN HOPPER and wife Geertie.
ANDRIES DE BAUN and wife Jannitje.

HARMAN VAN RYPEN and wife Maria.
JOHN G. ACKERMAN and wife Maria.
GEERTIE VAN BLERCOM, wife of David.
DAVID ACKERMAN, JR., and wife Jannitje.
ABRAHAM DEBAUN and wife Leah.
JOHN QUACKINBUSH and wife Annatie.
JOHN JANSEN and wife Sophia.
THOMAS D. ECKERSEN and wife Susanna.
DAVID ECKERSEN and wife Angenitie.
THOMAS I. ECKERSEN and wife Maria.
JACOB ECKERSEN and wife Annatie.
MARIA LABACH.
THOMAS ECKERSON and wife Cornelia.
LEAH TERHUNE, widow of Dirk.
ALBERT TERHUNE and wife Elisabeth.
JOHN TERHUNE and wife Catharina.
HENRY TERHUNE and wife Jannitje.
DAVID ACKERMAN and wife Antje.
DAVID HOPPER and wife Rachel.

WALDWICK METHODIST CHURCH
BERGEN COUNTY, NEW JERSEY

Rabaca of Peter Tebow of Bergen County and Susana, of Franklin County, b. Mar 22, 1797, bapt. Apr 23, 1797 by John Fountain, Minister.

Mary of Moris Sharp of Bergen County and Elesabeth of Franklin County, b. Apr 29, 1797, bapt. Apr 23, 1797, by John Fountain, Minister.

Hannah of Albert Wilson and Mary of Bergen County, b. Apr 16, 1796, bapt. Apr 24, 1796, by John Fountain, Minister.

Peter of Peter Tyse and Mary of Bergen County, b. Dec 29 1796, bapt. Mar 6, 1797, by John Fountain, Minister.

Samuel of Thomas Banton and Margaret of Bergen County, b. Nov 2, 1797, bapt. Dec 17, 1797 by John Clark, Minister.

James of Peter Ellye and Catrine of Bergen County, b. Nov 10, 1797, bapt. Dec 18, 1797 by John Seward, Minister.

William of Thomas Conklin and Charity of Bergen County, b. Nov 22, 1797, bapt. May 1, 1798, by John Clark, Minister.

Patty of Joseph Conklin of Rockland County and Hannah of Newhempsted, NY, b. Sep 13, 1792, bapt. May 1, 1793 by John Clark, Minister.

Matthias of Cornelius Conklin and Elizabeth of Bergen County, b. Jan 1, 1792, bapt. May 1, 1793, by John Clark, Minister.

Sary of Oliver Stevens and Susanna of Bergen County, b. Apr 10, 1795, bapt. Dec 2, 1797, by John Seward, Minister.

Cornelious of John Steavens and Susana of Bergen County, b. Apr 10, 1797, bapt. Jan 7, 1798, by John Seward, Minister.

Mary of John Smith and Rachel, of Bergen County, b. Feb 2, bapt. --- 17, 1798, by John Seward, Minister.

Lea of Peter Hopper and Detila of Bergen County, b. Jun 24, 1789, bapt. Feb 17, 1798 by John Seward, Minister.

Peter of Peter Hopper and Detila of Bergen County, b. Jul 12, 1793, bapt. Feb 17, 1798 by John Seward, Minister.

Charity of Peter Hopper and Detila of Bergen County, b. Jun 26, 1795, bapt. Feb 17, 1798 by John Seward, Minister.

Oliver of Daniel Odle and Hannah of Bergen County, b. Mar 22, 1786, bapt. Feb 17, 1798, by John Seward, Minister.

Oliver of Isack Firmin and Mary, b. Mar 10, 1797, bapt. May 14, 1798, by John Seward, Minister.

Mary of Peter Hopper and Detila, b. Sep 14, 1797, bapt. May 14, 1798, by John Seward, Minister.

Elisabeth of Benjamin Abrams and Sary, b. Mar 11, 1798, bapt. May 14, 1798, by John Seward, Minister.

John of William Badcock and Easter, b. Mar 15, 1798, bapt. May 14, 1798, by John Seward, Minister.

Barbay of William Badcock and Easter, b. Nov 25, 1795, bapt. May 14, 1798, by John Seward, Minister.

Hannah of John Smith and his wife, b. Apr 14, 1796, bapt. Jan 9, 1798 by John Seward, Minister.

Bety of Peter Hopper and his wife, b. Sep 29, 1797, bapt. Jan 9, 1798, by John Seward, Minister.

Fanny of Reuben Knap and his wife, b. Feb 12, 1797, bapt. May 16, 1798, by John Seward, Minister.

William N. of William M. Bell of Bergen County and Rachel of Franklin County, b. Jul 15, 1798, bapt. Aug 5, 1798, by John Clark, Minister.

Jane of Robart Cuddey and Ellander of Bergen County, b. Jul 25, 1798, bapt. Aug 5, 1798, by John Clark, Minister.

Archabil of Robart McCall and Elizabeth of Bergen County, b. May 16, 1798, bapt. Aug 5, 1798, by John Clark, Minister.

Elijay of James Stagg and Yaenne of Bergen County, b. Aug 16, 1798, bapt. Sep 2, 1798, by Samuel Thomas, Minister.

Harramanis of Vallintine Byard and Mary of Bergen County, b. Feb 26, 1796, bapt. Jun 6, 1798, by Samuel Thomas, Minister.

Andrew of Martin Graf and Corstana of Bergen County, bapt. Sep 30, 1798 by Samuel Thomas, Minister.

Polly of John Bakar and Betchsy of Bergen County, bapt. Oct 14, 1798, by James Tollesson, Minister.

Elizabeth of William Essex and Nancy of Bergen County, b. Apr 4, 1797, bapt. 1797 by John Fountain, Minister.

Mary of Samuel Forgisson and Jeny of Bergen County, b. 1800, bapt. Apr 27, 1800, by David Bertine, Minister.

John of Phillip Sloot and Sary of Bergen County, b. Sep 11, 1800, bapt. Sept 15, 1800, by Jesse Justis, Minister.

Margrit of James Bertulf of Bergen County and Leath of Newberdadus County, b. Nov 17, 1794, bapt. Oct 10, 1800 by Jesse Justis, Minister.

John of James Bertulf of Bergen County, and Leath of Hackinsack, b. Aug 28, 1799, bapt. Oct 10, 1800 by Jesse Justis, Minister.

Peter of Peter Tebow of Bergen County and Susana of Franklin County, b. Oct 3, 1800, bapt. Oct 26, 1800, by Joseph Totton,

Minister.

Thomas of James Stagg and Jantyne of Bergen County, Oct 10, 1800, Oct 26, 1800, by Joseph Totten, Minister.

John of Robbert Cuddy and Ellenor of Bergen County, b. 27 Oct 1800, bapt. 9 Nov 1800, by Joseph Totton, Minister.

Polly of Robert Macall and Elisabeth Macall of Bergen County, b. 1800, bapt. Nov 9, 1800 by Joseph Totton, Minister.

William of Peter Van Blarcom and Abygal of Bergen County, b. Dec 14, 1800, bapt. Jan 6, 1801, by Levey Moore, Minister.

Ayer of John Van Blarcom and Elsabeth of Bergen County, Oct 20, 1800, bapt. Jan 19, 1801, by Joseph Totton, Minister.

MINISTERS OF WALDWICK METHODIST CHURCH

Richard Whatcoat - 1791
John Fountain - 1797
Joseph Lovell - 1797
John Clark - 1797-1798
John Seward - 1797-1798
Samuel Thomas - 1798
James Tolleson - 1798-1799
Thomas Everheard - 1799

RAMAPO LUTHERAN CHURCH RECORDS
BERGEN COUNTY, NEW JERSEY
1750-1800

Church Book of the Ramapo Evangelical Lutheran Church began in the year 1750.

Births
Post - 1762
Jacob Post, b. Sep 21, 1762.
Catherine Post, b. Mar 3, 1765.
Susane Post, b. Jun 8, 1768.
Margreht Post b. Aug 26, 1770.

Conrath of Henry Goerlogh, b. Jun 16, 1764.
Simon of Henry Goerlogh, b. Sep 10, 1766.
Henry of Henry Goerlogh, b. Dec 29, 1768.
Adolf of Goerlogh, b. May 17, 1771. Godparents: Conrath
Brown and his wife, Anna.

Simon of Simon Rarch and his wife, Magdalene.

Henry of John Goerlogh and his wife, Elizabeth.
Adolf of Adolf Goergloch and his wife.

Dolly of Ditte Bowman, b. 1766.

Nicklass of Ditter Bowman, b. Feb 27, 1768. Godparents: Simon Karch
and Magdalena.
Michel of Ditter Bowman, b. Oct 10. Godparents: Michel Hore and his
wife, D.

Dolly of Fridrik Steyer, b. 1771. Godparents: William Wanemacker and
his wife.

Apr 1, 1770. Cunrad and Catharina [Hen]-selbekker fell in the heavy sin of the shame and begat a child. Altje van Boskerk also fell into the sin of fornication (Hurerey) and bore a son.

Consistory, Heinrich Brueckman retires, and in his place comes Hans Georg Achenbach. Heinrich Schuldes elected as Warden.

Feb 29, 1772. Hermanus Wannemacher retires as an elder, but is asked to remain as church master. Conrad Braun appointed as an elder. Warden (Vorstehre) Schneider proposed to replace Conrad Braun.

Feb 28, 1774. Hans Georg Achenbach retires as senior elder and is suceeded Heinrich Schultz in whose place as Warden was elected Anthony Krauter.

As elder Cunrad Braun now retires in whose place Adam Schneider and in his place as warden Hannes Henselbekker is proposed.

--- Storr, as an elder retires, Michel Storr chosen in his place. Cunrad Frederick chose as Warden.

BAPTISMS

Wannemecher's son Conraht, b. Aug 26, 1750, bapt. Oct 10, 1750. Wit: Conraht Meussinger and Conraht Friedrich's daughter, Maria.
Martin of Ary Dey, b. Oct 10, 1750, bapt. Jun 26. Wit: Martin Ross and his wife.

1751, April 14, was baptized Conraht Freussinger's son Pettrus the witnesses are Pitter Wannemacher and his wife.

1751, June 2, was baptized Daniel Korbman's daughter Cathrina. Witnesses Nicklass Meutssinger and his wife.

1751, June 2, was baptized Andross Bosskirch son Jacobus, the witnesses are Conraht Friedrich and his wife.

1751, June 2, was baptized Johannes Essler's daughter Anna, the witnesses are Conraht Freussinger and his wife. '

1751, June 2, was baptized Sam Sisscko daughter Salstohter the witnesses are Daniel Korbman and his wife.'

1751, August 11, was baptized Christian Wannemacher's son Adolph the witnesses are Adolph Schurt and his wife.

1749, December 18, was born Christian Wannemacher's son Dietrich.

1751, August 11, was baptized Wilhelm Remssis son Pettrus the witnesses are Pitter Wannemacher and his wife.

1751 August 11 was baptized Wilhelm Remssis daughter Maria the witnesses are Pitter Wannemacher and his wife.

1751 August 11 was baptized Christinn Zans daughter Susanna the witnesses are Jo Terbos and his wife.

1751 October 20 was baptized Thomas Wart's daughter ———— the witnesses are Petter Bulisfelt and ————

—— October 20 was baptized Hanss Van Winkels daughter ———— born 26 September the witnesses are Conraht Meussinger and ————

—— June 28 was baptized Conraht Frenssingers son Johannes the witnesses are Johannes Essler and his wife.

—— June 28 was baptized Robert Mathes' daughter Maria the witnesses are Davit Hinnion.

——June 28 was baptized Herman Gorg son Arend the witnesses are Arend DeGrand and his wife

—— September 24 was baptized Heinrich Wannemachers

---

1. Beginning in 1750, and until April 22, 1770 (twelve pages), the entries (with one or two exceptions), are in one handwriting (all in German), and in this form; 1750 den 10 tag October ist getausst worden Ary Dey sein sohn Martin und gebohren den 26 tag Juni die gezeugen sind Martin Ross und sein Weib. 1751, den 2 tag Juni ist getausst worden Daniel Korbmans tohter Cathrina die gezeugen sind Nicklass Meussinger und sein Weib. Thus *getaussi* is used for *getauft,* and *tohter* for *tochter* uniformly.

2. Qy: Sam Sisko's daughter Sal's daughter?

daughter Anna, the witnesses are Wilhelm Wannemacher and Anna Friedrich.

1755 June 1 was baptized Hanss Schuldes' son Mathes the witnesses are Mathes Barbaro and Catharina Meussinger

1755 June 1 was baptized Pitter Wannemacher's son Heinrich the witnesses are Christian Wannemacher and his wife.

1756 September 22 was baptized Hanse Van Winkels son Pettrus the witnesses are Gorg Gross and ———

1757 February 20 was baptized Wilhelm Wannemachers son Pettrus born January 20 the witnesses are Pitter Wannemacher and his wife

1757 February 20 was baptized Conraht Freussinger's son Conraht the witnesses are Johannes Essler and his wife

1757 February 20 was baptized Pitter Boss son Heinrich the witnesses are Heinrich Schueldes and Fronia Becher

1757 February 20 was baptized Ludwig Deringer's son Ludwig the witnesses are Ludwig Kammer and his wife

1757 May 8 was baptized Heinrich Fredrichs daughter Margaretta the witnesses are Conraht Friedrich and his wife

1757 May 22 was baptized Andreas Bosskerch's daughter ——— the witnesses are ———

1757 May 22 was baptized Heinrich Wannemacher's daughter Elissabeth the witnesses are Heinrich Friedrich and his wife

1757 May 2 was baptized Pitter Van Blarkum's son Antonia the witnesses are Elias Vally and his wife

1757 June 6 was baptized Johannes Schueldes son Johannes the witnesses are Simon ——— and his wife

1757 June 19 was baptized Conraht Friedrich's daughter Margaretha the witnesses are Conraht Friedrich and his wife

1757 August 27 was baptized Georg Becker's daughter Maria the witnesses are Conraht Wannemacher and his wife

1757 September 11 was baptized Georg Willers son Reinhart the witnesses are Reinhart Hanns and his wife.

1757 September 11 was baptized Hermanus Wannemacher's son Johannis born the 4th the witnesses are Pitter Bulisfield and his wife

1757 September 11 was baptized Mathes Barbaro's daughter Maria the witnesses are Jacob Becker and his wife

1757 November 6 was baptized Pitter Friedrich's son Heinrich the witnesses are Heinrich Wannemaker and his wife

1757 November 19 was baptized Philip Theise's daughter Anitye the witnesses are Philip Theise senior and his wife

1758 February 18 was baptized Robert Metes son Martin the witnesses are Georg Becker and his wife

1758 March 18 was baptized Adam Wannemacher's daughter Anitye the witnesses are Han Christ Goerlof and Margaretha Remise

1758 June 1 was baptized Johannes Roesch's daughter Maria born May 7th the witnesses are Dietrich Wannemacher and Maria Roesch

1760 ———— was baptized Harmanus Wannemacher's son ———— the witnesses are Wilhelm Wannemacher and his wife

———— ———— ———— Becker's son ———— the witnesses are Gorg Becker and his wife

1760 June 1 was baptized Simon Meyers son Martin born May 17 the witnesses are Cornelis Meyer and Catherina Meyer.

1760 June 1 was baptized Heinrich Emanuel's daughter Maria the witnesses are Conraht Braun and his wife

1760 June 1 was baptized Philip Fochs (?) daughter Catherina the witnesses are Martin Roesch and his daughter Maria.

1760 July 13 was baptized Jacob Sedler's son Johannis the witnesses are Johannis Theise and his wife

1760 August 25 was baptized Adam Wannemacher's son Christian the witnesses are Christian Wannemacher and his wife

1760 September 7 was baptized Johannes Streter's son Johann Jost the witnesses are Jost Miller and Elizabeth Frenssinger

1760 September 15 was baptized Tohmas Von Bosskerch's daughter Lea the witnesses are Georg Firman and his wife

1760 October 19 was baptized Heinrich Friedrich's daughter Rahel the witnesses are Abraham von Bosskerch and his wife

1760 November 16 was baptized Lawrenss Cobuss Von Bosskerch's son Laurenss the witnesses are Heinrich Friedrich and his wife

1760 November 16 was baptized Johannis Schaeffer's daughter Maria the witnesses are Jacob Becker and his wife

1760 November 16 was baptized Christian Kraufts son Christian the witnesses are Johannis Becker and his wife

1760 November 30 was baptized Michel Fischer's son Michel the witnesses are Simon Karch and his wife

1761 January 11 was baptized Johannis Hensselbecker's son Michel the witnesses are Johannis Theise and his wife

1761 January 24, was baptized Johannis Hansen's daughter Christina the witnesses are Reinhart Hansen and his wife

1761 May 11 was baptized Isaac Mont——— son Isaac the witnesses are Dominie Graaf ———

1761 May 31 was baptized Adolf Goerlochs son Johannis the witnesses are Pittor Pulisfeldt and wife

The other son Hermanus the same day the witnesses are Hermanus Wannemacher and his wife

1761 May 24 was baptized Conraht Braun's daughter Anna Margrethe the witnesses are Simon Kerch and wife Magdalena.

1761 July 19 was baptized Conraht Friedrich's son Jacob the witnesses are Jost Van Boskirch and his wife Elizabeth

1761 August 2 was baptized Wilham Ekhard's daughter Elizabeth born July 19 the witnesses are Hanss Gorg Gebel and wife Ofilea

1761 August 16 was baptized Reinhard Hausse's son Johann Jacob the witnesses are Johann Jacob Trember and sister Elizabeth

1761 August 16 was baptized Hermann Gorg's son Jacobus the witnesses are Hermanus DeGrau and sister Maria.

1761 August 30 was baptized Philip Teisse daughter Cathrina the witnesses are Jacobus Forshss (Fochss) and his wife Cathrina

1761 October 23 was baptized Georg Firmans son Gorrg the witnesses are Pitter Von Der Burg and his wife Abal———

1761 October 23 was baptized Jacobus Fochs's daughter Maria the witnesses are Philip Teisse and his wife Margaret

1761 November 8 was baptized Conraht Meussinger's daughter Catherina the witnesses are Wilhelm Wannemacher and his wife

1761 November 22 was baptized Matheys Barbaro his daughter Elizabeth the witnesses are Conraht Freusinger and his wife

1761 November 23 was baptized George Beckers daughter ——————— the witnesses are Wilhelm Wannamacher and his wife

1762 February —— was baptized Pitter Boss's son (David ?) the witnesses are Ludwig Crammar and his wife

1762 March —— was baptized Pitter Wannemacher's daughter ——————· the witnesses are Jost Shurt and his wife

1762 May 30 was baptized Heinrich Wannemacher's son Abraham the witnesses are Hermanus Wannemacher and wife Susanne

1762 July 18 was baptized Heinrich Goerloh's daughter Elshe the witnesses are Christian Goerloh and his mother Elshe

1762 February 15 was baptized Johannes Teise daughter Catherina the witnesses are Friedrich Teise and his wife Anke

1762 August 2 was baptized Robert Hunter's daughter Anna the witnesses are Hannes Teise and his wife

1762 August 2 was baptized Hans Georg Knauss' son Jacob the witnesses are Johannes Sinselbah and wife Elizabeth

1762 September 12 was baptized Johannes Becker's son Matthes the witnesses are Matthes Barbaro and wife Margrethe

1762 September 7 was baptized Niklas De Gran's Jannica the witnesses are Arent De Gran and wife Elizabeth

1762 December 19 was baptized Johannes Schaeffer's son Jacob the witnesses are Adam Becker and Maria Freussinger

1762 December 19 was baptized Joseph Conklen's son John the witnesses are John Conklen and wife Catherina

1763 January 30 was baptized Heinrich Schuldes' daughter Maria the witnesses are Conraht Boss and Maria Roesch

1763 February 13 was baptized Jacob Knauss son Jacob the witnesses John Conklen and his wife

1763 July 3 was baptized Pittor Friedrich's son Tohmes the witnesses are Thomas Bosskirch and wife Maria

1763 August 14 was baptized Jacob Horn's son Jacob the witnesses are Jacob Becker and wife Elizabeth

1763 August 14 was baptized Jost Miller's son Johann Goerg the witnesses are Ludwig Schumacher and Georg Miller's wife.

1763 September 10 was baptized Adam Schneider's daughter Catherina the witnesses are Heinrich Brickman and wife Catherina

1763 September 11 was baptized Conraht Meussinger's son Niklass the witnesses are Heinrich ———— and his wife Margerethe

1763 October 9 was baptized Antoni Krauter's son Pettrus the witnesses are Johannes Kertz and wife Anna

1763 November 20 was baptized Conraht Friedrich's daughter Elizabeth the witnesses are Heinrich Wannemacher and wife

1763 December 4 was baptized Ludwig Bruekman's son Jacob the witnesses are Jacob Bruekman and wife Catherina

1763 December 18 was baptized Reinhart Bruckman's son Jacob the witnesses are Jacob Bruckman and his wife

1764 January 8 was baptized Georg Baumann's daughter Catherina the witnesses are Johannes Sterter and wife Cathrina

1764 January 8 was baptized Willem Eckhard's son Jacob the witnesses are Jacob Baumann and wife

1764 March 4 was baptized Jacob Knauss' daughter Elizabeth the witnesses are Heinrich Wannemacher and wife Elizabeth

1764 March 18 was baptized Johannes Theisen son Johannes the witnesses are Pittor Theisen's son Johannes and Elizabeth Storr

1764 March 18 was baptized Jacobus Hanssen's son Davit the witnesses are Willem Schinlen and his wife

1764 March 18 was baptized Willem Cuerter's daughter Elizabeth the witnesses are John Schinken and his wife

1764 September 2 was baptized Marmaduck ———— —— Marmaduck the witnesses are Steven Schlod and his wife

1764 November 25 was baptized Willem Wannemacher's daughter Maria the witnesses are Heinrich Fueseh and his wife

1764 November 25 was baptized Willem Ran's son Willem the witnesses are Willem Henselbecker and his wife

1764 December 23 was baptized Simon Meyer's daughter Yainthe the witnesses are Jacobus Fuesch and his wife

1765 February 3 was baptized Maria Braun the witnesses are Simon Meyer and Maria Wilsson

1765 February 17 was baptized Pitter Friedrichs son John the witnesses are John Concklen and his wife

1765 April 14 was baptized Andreas Bulisfeld's daughter Sussanna the witnesses are Hermanus Wannemaker and his wife

1765 April 14 was baptized Jost Miller's daughter Elizabeth the witnesses are Hans Georg Gebel Junior and Elizabeth Gebel

1765 April 22 was baptized Pittor Post's daughter Cathrina the witnesses are Heinrich Brueckman and wife Cathrina

1765 May 12 was baptized Johannis Shuerts son Conraht the witnesses are Conraht Freussinger and wife Elizabeth

1765 May 25 was baptized Reinhard Hanssen's son Thomas the witnesses are Heinrich Fuesch and wife

1765 June 16 was baptized Pittor Theisen's son Conrath the witnesses are Conrath Storr and his wife

1765 July 28 was baptized Nicklas Goerloh's daughter Anna the witnesses are Conrath Wanemacher and his wife

1765 July 28 was baptized Willem Schinken's son Joseph the witnesses are Johannes Braun and his wife

1765 November 17 was baptized Johannes Sterter's son Jonas the witnesses are Jonas Miller and his daughter

1765 December 24 was baptized Jacob Knauss's son Conrath the witnesses are Conrath Friedrich and his wife Margrethe

1765 December 29 was baptized Antoni Kranter's daughter Anna the witnesses are Jacobus Berleman and his sister Anhe

1766 February 9 was baptized Jost Shuert's daughter 'Margrethe the witnesses are Pittor Wannemacher and wife

1766 March 31 was baptized Heinrich Herbet's son Heinrich Willem the witnesses are Willem Ran and his wife Barbara

1766 April 13 was baptized Willem Winter's daughter Hester the witnesses are John Concklen and wife Cathrina

1766 April 13 was baptized Adam Wannemacker's daughter Margretta the witnesses are Heinrich Goerloh and wife Margretta

1766 May 11 was baptized Ludwig Bruckman's daughter Cathrina the witnesses are Heinrich Brueckman and wife Cathrina

1766 July 13 was baptized Hermanus Wannemacher's son ———— the witnesses are Andreas Bulisfeld and his wife

1766 December 14 was baptized John Schuken's daughter Cathrina the witnesses are James Serven and ————

1767 January 8 was baptized Conrath Lishier's daughter Maria the witnesses are Reinhart Brueckman and wife Wilhelmina

1767 February 8 was baptized Simon Hass' daughter Cathrina the witnesses are Johannes Hass and wife Cathrina

1767 April 17 was baptized Conrath Raby's son Conrath the witnesses are Conrath Raby and his wife

1767 April 18 was baptized Conrath Boss' daughter Margretta the witnesses are Pitter Boss and his wife

1767 April 18 was baptized Johannes Goerloh's daughter Cathrina the witnesses are Nicklas Schueldes and his wife

1767 May 27 was baptized Jacob Himmion's son Adam the witnesses are Adam Himmion Fredrich Reiss and Sophia

1767 June 7 was baptized Simon Meyer's daughter Henrica the witnesses are Henrich Brueckman and his wife

1767 July 23 was baptized Jacob Becker's daughter Cathrina the witnesses are Heinrich Brueckman and wife Cathrina

1767 July 26 was baptized Davit Henion's son Daniel the witnesses are Pitter Henion and his wife

. 1767 September 7 was baptized Christ Goerloh's son Johann Georg the witnesses are Conrath Meussinger and his wife

1767 November 1 was baptized Antonio Krauter's daughter Elizabeth the witnesses are father and mother

1767 November 1 was baptized Hans Henion's daughter Lenna the witnesses are Davit Henion and his wife

1767 December 25 was baptized Conrath Meussinger's son Conrath the witnesses are Hermanus Wannemaker and ——

1768 January —— was baptized Johannes Shnert's daughter Elizabeth the witnesses are Pitter Wannamacher and wife Maria

1768 January 3 was baptized Reinhard Hanss' son Christian the witnesses are Pitter Boss and his daughter ——

1768 March 2 was baptized Pitter Boss' daughter Maria the witnesses are Heinrich Schueldes and wife Maria

1768 June 19 was baptized Ludwig Kraut's daughter Elizabeth the witnesses are father and mother

1768 August 23 was baptized Johannes Theiss's Junior's daughter Maria the witnesses are Pitter Theisse and his wife Maria

1768 October 9 was baptized Willem Winder's son Lues the witnesses are Lues Concklen and his sister Rachel

1767   Baldes Shoonmackers son John Jacob is christen
                  12th 1767 and borne Jann 10th 1767 the god-
father   Hennion Jacob Himmon Steven Himmon
wife

1768 October 9 was baptized Conrath Braun's son Heinrich the witnesses are Heinrich Brueckman and wife Cathrina

1768 October 9 was baptized Ludwig Brueckman's son Johannes the witnesses are father and mother

1768 November 6 was baptized Willem Hensselbecker's

Magdalena the witnesses are Conrath Hensselbecker and Elizabeth Storr

1768 December 18 was baptized Jost Schuert's son Joseph the witnesses are Paulus Redan and his wife

1769 February 19 was baptized Corneliss Lischier's daughter Cathrina the witnesses are Heinrich Brueckman and his wife

1769 March 5 was baptized Philip Jung's son Johann Heinrich the witnesses are Adam and Heinrich Hennion and Baltes Schueldes

1769 March 10 was baptized Han Christ Goerloh's daughter Maria the witnesses are Willem Remsse and sister Maria

1769 March 6 was baptized Michel Redman's son Johannes the witnesses are Johannes Bayer and his wife

1769 March 24 was baptized Reinhard Brueckman's son Heinrich the witnesses are Heinrich Brueckman and his wife

1769 March 24 was baptized Hermanus Wannemacher's son Hermanus the witnesses are Conrath Meussinger and

1769 February 20 was baptized Conrath Raby's son Jacob the witnesses are Elias Vally and his wife

1769 March 24 was baptized Adam Wannemacher's daughter Elizabeth the witnesses are Johannis Goerloh and his wife

1769 April 23 was baptized Joseph Concklen's son James the witnesses are father and mother

1769 July 9 was baptized Conrath Fredrich's son Heinrich the witnesses are Heinrich Fredrich and wife Margretta

1769 July 9 was baptized Johannes Henion's son Abraham the witnesses are Abraham Henion

1769 July 9 was baptized Adam Henion's son Johann Heinrich the witnesses are Heinrich Henion and Philip Inng's wife

1769 August 6 was baptized Stephen Henion's son Johannes the witnesses are Johannes Bayer Jacob Hennion and Georg Henion and his wife Charlotte

1769 September 3 was baptized Jacobus Meyer's daughter

Magdalena the witnesses are Adolf Meyer and wife

1769 September 17 was baptized Antoni Krauter's son Jacob the witnesses are father and mother

1769 October 15 was baptized Pitter Vally's daughter Maria the witnesses are Conrath Braun and wife Anne

1769 October 29 was baptized Conrath Meussinger's son Conrath the witnesses are Conrath Wannemacher and Henrich Wannemacher's daughter

1769 November 26 was baptized Davit Degrot's daughter Arianna the witnesses are Albert Cornell and his wife

1769 December 23 was baptized Pitter Storr his son Jacob the witnesses are Jacob Storr and his wife

1769 December 24 was baptized Willem Rou his son Johann Philip the witnesses are Philip Henselbeck and Conrath Storr's daughter

1770 January 26 was baptized Simon Meyer's daughter Cathrina and born the 20: the witnesses are Gotfried ———— and wife Cathrina

1770 March 18 was baptized Diedrich Wannemacher's son Pitter the witnesses are Pitter Wannemacher and Cornelis Bante's daughter

1770 April 15 was baptized Georg Himmion's daughter Maria Elizabeth the witnesses are Baldes Schumacher's wife Philip Yung's wife and Adam and Henrich Himmion.

1770 April 22 was baptized Isaac Madanien son Henrich born the 23 March Witnesses Heinch G———— and his wife

1770.

Parentes	Infantes	Sponsors
Cunrad Henselbekker	Johan Wilhelm	Wilhelm Hensel-
N. V. Uxor	May 13	bekker & uxor
	d	
	Jun 2	
William Winter	Conrath	Conrath Horr
Elizabeth — —	Chrisent July 22-1770	Magdalena
Litter Capenfelt	Henry	Henry esler
N. N. — —	Chisent July 22-1770	Catharina King
1769		
David Kedman	Dorethe	Jacob Hertz
Christina	borne June 3	Dorethe
Adam Himmion	John Baldefer	Baldefer Schuman
Sophia	Crisent august 19-1770	his wife
Reinhard Hause	anna Margretha 1770	faether
Margretha — —	Crisent September 2 born July 13	
		Mother
Ditter Bos	John Reinhard	Reinhard Brickman
Margrehta	Crisent September 16-1770	
		Wilhelmina
David Bayer	anna Maria	John Bayer
anna	Crisent September 16 1770	his wife
Nicklas goerlogh	elizabeth	Henry Wannemac—
elizabeth	Crisent october 28 1770	elizabeth
George Backer	Jacob	Conrath Wannema—

1. The following records are in English, in an entirely different hand from the preceding. They are given herewith precisely as written.

Maria	Crisent october 28 1770	Catherina
John weber	eliza Barbara	father
N. v.	Crisent November 25 1770.	Mother
Lembel Jumens	Magdalena borne 24 octo	Simon kargh
Mary	Crisent November 27 1770	Magdelena
Andreas Pulesfelt	Mary borne Novem 19	Pitter Pelesf
Cornelia	Crisent december 23 1770	and his wife
Henry Himmion	Cathrina	George Himmion
Magdalena	Crisent december 26 1770	Charlotte
Joseph Concklen	William	William Concklen
elizabeth	Crisent december 26 1770	n. v.
William Rauld	Cathrina	John Ros
Dorethe	crisent Janna 6 1771	Cathrina Becker
John Thise	Margretha	Philip Thise
Maryrethe	Crisent Janna 20 born Dec. 20 1770	
John Concklen	John — —	father and
Cathrina	Crisent Jann 11—1771	mother
Ludwig Brickman	Willhelmina	Remhard Brickman
Coa	Crisent March 29 1771	Wilhelmina
David Degrot	Nancy	His sister
Hencke	Crisent June 28 1771	
Antony krauter	Mary	Michel Weyman
Cathrina	Crisent July 14 1771	his wife
William Henselbacker	Margretha	Philip Henselback
Cathrina	Crisent July 14 1771	Margretha Stor
Luwes Concklon	Luwes	Luiwes Schoort
Mary	Crisent July 28 1771	anna esler
Kerhard Brickman	Pettrus	Pitter Bos
Wihelmina	Crisent august 11 1771	Margretha
Jacobus Meyer	Jannycke	father and
	Crisent october 6 1771	Mother
Hermanes wannemackerthomes borne June 8		Henry Redener
Susana	Crisent June 12 1771	Mary
Christian goerlogh	Davit	Davit Redman
Ane	Crisent November 3 1771	Christina
George Darleman	Mary borne oct. 2	Isaac Maurese
Mary	Crisent November 17 1771	Mary
Henry Scholdes	Lodwig born feber 26	Conrath Bos

Mary   Crisent Mach 31 1771   elesbeth

1771 John Goerloh   Mary born Sept 4 Pitter Wannemaker

elizabeth   Crisent Sept 22   Mary

1771 Jost Schoort   william   William Schoort

Lidia   Crisent december 25   his wife

1771 David Redman   Mary born august 19 Michel Redman

Christina   Crisent September 8   Cathrina

1772

1772 Conrath Henselbacker   John   Johannes Henselbecker

anna   Crisent Jannewary 5   eva

1772 Andrew Meyer   Crisent feber 2   Jannathe

John Conrath   Conrath Henselba—

1772 Pitter Ratan   Crisent feber 16   anna

1772 William Rauw   Mary   Henry Brickman

Dorethe   John   John Meyer

Jamathe   Crisent March 1   Cathrina

1772 John teyse Junier   Jacob born feber 2   Jacob Storr

elizabeth   Crisent March 1   Margretha

1772 Henry Rednar   Margreth Hermanus Wanne[maker]

Mary   Crisent May 17   Susanna

1772 Jacob Bilju   Janatha born March 29 John von Law

Jannathe   Crisent May 17   engelhe

1772 William winter   Johannes   John teyse

elizabeth   Crisent May 17   Margreth

1772 Christian Bules   Jacob born May 20   albert ackerman

Clara   Crisent June 8   anne

1772 Philip yung   anne Cathrina   Baldes Schoonmaker

Margreth   Crisent June 8   Cathrina

1772 Reinhard House   William   father and

Margareth   Crisent october 11   Mother

1772 Conrath friedrik   John   John van Boske—

Mary   Crisent october 25   Rachel

1772 Dietrick Thesse   abraham born November 5

Christian Bules

anne   Crisent December 6   Clara

1772 Henry Scholdes   elizabeth   ● Reinhard Brickman

Mary   Crisent december 29   Wilhelmina

1773 William Henselbacker   William borne dec. 22   Michel Stor

Cathrina	Crisent Janna 3	Dorothe
Philipp Ekert	Abigail born Dec. 16th 1771	
		Jacob Ekert
Catharina	Crisent Jan. 29 1773	and wife
Henry Strabel	Elizab. Margrethe b. Dec. 23 1772	
		Peter Strabel
Catharine	Cristen Jan. 29 : 1773 Goth. Gebhard	
		Margareth Strabel
1773 Pitter Poss	elizabeth born Jann 16th	
		Reinhard Brickman
elizabeth	Crisent feber 14th	Wilhelmina
1773 Henry Bullesfeld	Jacobus born feber 5th	Adolf goerlogh
Cornelia	Chrisent feber 28th	anna
John Evergman	John	Lem Yumer
N. N.	b. January 25th	& wife
	c: 5th March 1770	
1773 John Goerlogh	John Henry born March 8th	
elizabeth	Chrisent March 19	Henry Mills
1773 John Weber	Mary	father
N. N.	Chrisent March 28th	Mother
1773 Pitter Hanion	Margarethe born Jann: 8th	
		William Jenkins
N. N.	Chrisent March 28th	Margarethe
1773 Friik Steyer	Mary born March 23th	William Kansy
elshe	Chrisent April 9th	Mary
1773 Cornelis Leizier	Rebecca born March 6th	Adam Sn—
Jannathe	Chrisent April 11th	Dorothe
1773 Philip yung	Cathrina elenora	George Dimion
Margreth	Chrisent May 30th Jacob Himion wife	
1773 Adam Himion	John born July 2th	John Spros
Sophia	Chrisent august 5th Cathrina Sprosm	
1773 Philip Henselbacker	John	Johannis Henselbe—
Margretha	Chrisent august 15th	eva
1773 George Bochman	Margreth born 26 July	Jacob ——
Mary — —	Chrisent august 15th	his wife
1773 Davit Redman	Jacob Philip	Michel Red—
Christina	Chrisent october 24th	his wife
1773 Davit Henion	Jannathe	father

	Cathrina	Chrisent october 24th Mother
1773	George Backer	Margreth Ludewig Shu——
	Mary	Chrisent November 7th Margreth Shu
1773	Jacobus Myer	abraham goetus
		Chrisent November 7th
1773	John teebout	anna Maria born october 27th
		John philip
	eva	Chrisent December 5th Maria east
		Domminicus and
		Barbara east
1773	Henry goerlogh	george born october 5th Nicklas goer—
	Margreth	Chrisent November 1th elizabeth
1773	William winter	Haty Michel Stor—
	elizabeth	Chrisent December 19th Margreth Sto
1773	Abel Redner	Susane born Henry Redner
		Chrisent December 24th Mary —— —
1773	Simon Myer	arianhe born December 10
		Cornelis My——
	Jannathe	Chrisent December 24th arianhe
1774	Reinhard Brickman	Catharina born Dec 22
		John Conke
	Wilhelmina	Chrisent Janna 16th Cathrina
1774	Pitter Ramsy	William born December 26th father
		Chrisent Jann 16th Mother
1774	Conrath Henselbacker	elizabeth Pitter ———
	anna	Chrisent Jann 30 Margreth ——
1774	william vally	annathe borne March 18th father
	anna	Chrisent Appril 8th and anna Bam—
1774	John Rednar	John born appril 1th Abele Rig——
	Nancy	Chrisent Appril 17th his wife ——
1774	Lodewig Kraut	Cathrina Dorethe Nicklas ———
	Phebe	Chrisent august 26th aCathrina
1774	Jost Shourt	william John Concklen
	Liedia	Chrisent august 28th Cathrina
1774	Joseph Brown	John father and
	Sare	Chrisent august 28th Mother
1774	Christian goerlogh	John born Septe 28th John goerlogh
	ahe	Chrisent october 17th elizabeth

1760	Michel Weymer	Jacob born September 13th	Parents
	Mary		
1765	Mihel Weymer	edward born July 24th	Parents
	Mary		
1769	Michel Weymer	George born December 22th	Parents
	Mary		
1772	Michel Weymer	annige born feber 15th	Parents
	Mary		
1774	Michel Weymer	Jacobus born July 1st antony Kraut	
	Mary	Cathrina	
1779	Michel weymer	Johnny born September 9th	Parents
	Mary		
1774	Conrath Meusinger	Michel Born March the 13	Michel Stor
	Margretha	Chrisent Appril 4th	
1774	anntony Krauter	Jacobus	Jacobus Barleman
	Cathrina	Chrisent appril 4th	his wife
1774	adam Himion	anna Magdalena	Stiven Himion
	Sophia	Chrisent November 20th	his wife
1774	**William Henselbacker**	**Cathrina born Nov 14**	
			John Rose
	Cathrina	**Chrisent Dec 4th**	**Cathrina**
1774	Hanloery fox	Henry	Philip tissa
	Henriha	Chrisent December 4th	Margrethe
1775	Reinhard House	elizabeth born august 24th	
			Philip fox
	Margreth	Chrisent September 17th	elizabeth
"	John von Law	John	Pitter Ramsy
	engelhe	Chrisent September 17th	his wife
"	David Redman	Magdalena born august 15th	
			fridrih grime
	Christina	Chrisent September 17th	Barbara
"	John von Boskerk	andres born September 17th	
			andres Boskerk
	Sara	Chrisent october 15th and his Mother	
"	Isaac Sisko	Janathe	Pitter Hannabal
		Chrisent october 23	Marg
"	John Rose	Jacob born November 15th	
			John henselbacker

Cathrina	Chrisent December 21	eve
1776 John Rose.	John William born feber 17	
		William Henselbacker
Cathrina	Chrisent April 24th	Cathrina
" Jacobus fox	andres	father and
Cathrina	Chrisent April 24th	Mother
" thomas Boogs	elizabeth	John goerlogh
Cathrina	Chrisent April 24th	elizabeth
" abraham v Buskerk	David born November 7th 1775	
		David v Boskerk
Iea	Chrisent April 24th	Rachel
1775 Christian Pules	Daniel born Febr 23th Conrath Pules	
Clara	Chrisent March 19th	eva
" John Goerlogh	William born March 1th Domini Gra-	
elizabeth	Chrisent March 19th	Barbara
" Andres Bules	Cornelia born March 10th Henry ——	
Cornelia	Chrisent April 2th	Cornelia
" Pitter fridrik	John godfrid	John Godfrid
		Nicklas Har——
	Chrisent april 2th	and his wife
" Luwes Concklen	Charety	Nicklas Lishe
Mary	Chrisent april 16th	Charety
" Cornelis von Horne	Christina Rosina	John Roesh
abia	Chrisent, May —th	Rosina
" Pitter Ratan	Jannathe born — abram von Boskerk	
Jannathe	Chrisent July —	Lea
1776 John Concklen	Cathrina born June 24th Petter Fri	
Cathrina	Chrisent November 10th	Moly
" Lewis Conklen	John born September 21th	
		Henry esler
Mary	Chrisent November 10th	
		and his Mother
" william Dey	Petter born october 13th Petter Hame	
	Chrisent November 10th	Mary
" Conrad Henselbaker		Michel Stor
anna	Chrisent November 10th	Dorothe
" william vally	elias born June 2th	Conrath Rapp
anna	Chrisent July 23th	Clara

" Christina goèrlogh abraham borne october 16
           Henry Brickman
 ahe   'Chrisent Nove 10th
           Cathrina Brickman
     Magdalena Dito John Goerlogh
          elizabeth goerlogh
1776 Conrath Meusinger Margreth   Jacob Stor
 Margreth   Chrisent May 26th Margreth
" Adam Sneider Janathe   Cornelis Lizer
 Dorethe   Chrisent May 26th Jannathe
" William Henselbaker Jacob born october 10th Jacob Stor
 Oathrina   Chrisent November 10th Margreth
" Jost Miller   Marg born octo 3th Johnathan traph
 Cathrina   Chrisent November 10th Cathrina
" antony krauter   father
 Maria (?) Chrisent November 10th and Mother
1774 Henry Scholdes Henry   father and
 Mary   Chrisent august 2th Mother
" Henry labach Henry born Janna 15th Henry Mande
 Margreth   Chrisent feber 8th Dorothe
1775 Dirck Wannemacker Margretha Conrath fox
 Margreth   Chrisent Janna 22th Margreth
" Albert ackerman gerret born Jann 18th Michel Stor
 anhe   Chrisent feber 5th Margreth Stor
1770 John Redner Henry born May 5th Henry Redner
 Nancy   Chrisent May 26th Mary
1772 John Redner Pitter born appril 9th Pitter Poss
 Nancy   Chrisent appril 14th elizabeth
1775 Jost Degrot   Rehert born 4th october 1772 father
 elizabeth   Chrisent March 18th and polly willis
" Jost Degrot   elizabeth born Janna 22th
           Jacobus Degrot
 elizabeth   Chrisent March 18— Jannathe
1778 Lodewig fisher elizabeth borne May 4th
           John goerlogh
 Polly   Chrisent June 8th elizabeth goer—
" John Rose   Cathrina   Henry Brickman
 Cathrina   Chrisent June 8th Cathrina Brickman

1779	Gerret Blawfelt	John	Pitter quacken— —
	Margreth	Chrisent March 13th	
			Margreth quack—
	Mathew Bensen	John	John Banta,
		Chrisent March 13th	and his wife
		Dirck Ditto	Dirck wannemaker
			and his wife
"	william folly	elizabeth borne feber 16th	father
	anna	Chrisent March 14th	and Mother
"	Henry Reydenauer	Henry	
	elizabeth	Chrisent March 14th	
"	Henry goerlogh	Mathew Leonart Herm—	
	Margreth	Chrisent March 13th anna Herm—	
"	Henry Rittner	Elizabeth b. Dec. 7th 1774 Wm Bi—	
			& —
	Marya	Marya b. June 20th 1779 Henry Bi—	
			& Nancy —
"	David Baldewin	thomes	thomes Boskerck
	Rachel	Chrisent October 31th	Marya
"	John Storm	Margrethe born Sept 24th Petter Boss	
	Cathrina	Chrisent October 30th : Margreth	
"	John von Law	Sara born december 4th 1778	
	engelhe	Chrisent October 31	
"	Antony krauter	Edward born 26 october Jost depone	
		Chrisent october 31 and his wife	
1780	thomes Boogs	elizabeth : John goerlogh	
	Cathrina	Chrisent May 21th elizabeth	
"	Petter Fechee	Rebecka born March 31th	
			Petter Lezeer
	Mary	Chrisent May 21th Rebeca	
"	John georg fox	Henry father and	
		Chrisent May 21th Mother	
1781	william wannemaker	margreath J— Wannemaker	
		crissent born	
	Susanna	august 39 Polly Brown	
	Jacob Banda	Leona born october 11 John —	
			His wife

"   Petter Bomen   Margrit March 26   .   Wilhelm
                                                        wannemaker
                                                        Margrit
1784 William Wannamaker   born   Conrate
                                                        Brown
                          crissent conrate is 28 april   anty
"   William fally   mary was   henry ridner
                          born 21 of august   mary ridner
"   William fally   david was   ————
                          born 2 march   ————

1786 William Wannamaker
     his son Harmanus was
     Born 24 December

1768 Conrad Brown his son   ————
     Henry was born 16
     day September   ————

1787 Polly Brown hur daugh-   Coon
ter was Born 21 day of July Nansey   and ————

1789 William Wannamaker   Henry ————
     his Son was Henry was   and
     born 13 September 1789   Mary

1765 Coonroat Brown .   Mary born 7 May   ————
     and his wife Mary .   . ————

1792 William Wanamaker   Henry ——
     his Daughter Anchea.   Bro———
     was born the 12 October   and
     Chrisent 14 : 1792   ————

1791 Thomas Jonas his   Tho——
     Daughter was born in .
     the year, 1791   .
     ————obard Jonas his   Rob——
     Daughter .   ————
     (Torn out)   Wannamaker
                       ——ghter ————

—87 John Ross his son Frad-   Conroat
     rick was born 5th Aug-   —— . .   Brown
     ust.

Heritage Books by F. Edward Wright: